Vietnam Anthology

Vietnam Anthology: American War Literature

Nancy Anisfield, Editor

Bowling Green State University Popular Press
Bowling Green, Ohio 43403

Photography—Chad Harter/Studio 5, © 1969
Design—Nancy Anisfield

Acknowledgements

Excerpt from *One Very Hot Day* copyright © 1967 by David Halberstam. Reprinted by permission of the author.

Excerpt from *Dog Soldiers* by Robert Stone. Copyright © 1973 by Robert Stone. Reprinted by permission of Houghton Mifflin Company.

Excerpt from *The Alleys of Eden* copyright © 1981 by Robert Olen Butler. Reprinted by permission of the author.

From *The 13th Valley* by John Del Vecchio. Copyright © 1982 by John M. Del Vecchio. Reprinted by permission of Bantam Books, Inc.

Stephen Wright, excerpted from *Meditations in Green*. Copyright © 1983 Stephen Wright. Reprinted with the permission of Charles Scribner's Sons.

"Major Bedford's Career" from *Lieutenant Kit* by Jeff Danziger, reprinted by permission of the author.

"The Interrogation of the Prisoner Bung by Mister Hawkins and Sergeant Tree" originally appeared in *Esquire*. Reprinted by permission of David Huddle.

"The Ambush" by Asa Baber. First published in *The Falcon* © 1972. Used by permission of the author.

"Thi Bong Dzu" by Larry Lee Rottmann, first appeared in the anthology *Free Fire Zone: Short Stories by Vietnam Veterans*, published by 1st Casualty Press/McGraw-Hill, 1973.

"The Homecoming" from *The Wind Shifting West* by Shirley Ann Grau. Copyright 1973 by Shirley Ann Grau. Reprinted by permission of Brandt & Brandt Literary Agents, Inc.

"The First Clean Fact" from *Paco's Story* by Larry Heinemann. Copyright © 1979, 1980, 1981, 1984, 1986 by Larry Heinemann. Reprinted by permission of Farrar, Straus and Giroux, Inc.

"Wingfield" © 1981 by Tobias Wolff. From *In the Garden of North American Martyrs* by Tobias Wolff, published by The Ecco Press in 1981. Reprinted by permission.

Contents

Preface

Although the body of literature written by Americans about the war in Vietnam is fairly recent, it is surprisingly extensive and diversified. As with all anthologies, then, this collection required careful selection and arrangement. The first task was to determine the scope of the text, and it quickly became apparent that limiting the works to those written by Americans was necessary. If fiction and poetry by Vietnamese as well as writers of other nationalities were included, it would be nearly impossible to draw any conclusions about the literature and its significance; the variety would be overwhelming and any kind of focus would be inaccessible. By including only works by American authors, we can at least learn what this confusing war was like for Americans. Furthermore, by narrowing the scope of the anthology, the literature presented here can be read in a context, put in its place in the rich tradition of American war literature.

The next main criteria for inclusion (besides availability) were variety and literary merit—an ambiguous term which I roughly define as the characteristic of having interpretive value on more than one level. Many of the pieces selected have appeared on the syllabi of college level Vietnam War literature and history courses across the country, which is as close a mark of canonization as may be possible for a literature only twenty years old.

Some of the finest writings to come out of the war are non-fiction: personal narratives, memoirs, and oral histories. Despite the resonance factual accounts often have—that startling realization that what is read is real—their factuality usually precludes literary analysis. It's hard to dispute contradictions in a character or evaluate the timing of a climactic event when they are fact, rather than artistic creation. Hence personal narratives were excluded from this collection, although several of the most powerful and engrossing works written so far are non-fiction.

While this anthology is intended for use as a primary text in war literature courses and a secondary text in history courses, my judgments were guided by the sensibilities of an English teacher, not a politician or historian. There may be, therefore, an imbalance in political tone or the time and location of some of the pieces. Because of the desire to provide as wide a variety of narrative styles, poetic voices, and images

1

as possible, politics and historical coverage were deemed secondary. This book, as opposed to history and political science texts, presents the Vietnam experience through the creative expression of various men and women whose lives were changed by the war. A literary approach also lent itself most simply to division by genre; as a result the segments are broken down into novel excerpts, short stories, poetry, and drama.

As a primary text for courses focusing on the literature of this war, *Vietnam Anthology* offers a sampling of fiction and poetry by veterans and non-veterans, seasoned writers and those who used their war experience as an incentive to begin writing. Hopefully the book will serve as a springboard, propelling students deeper into the literature; novel excerpts are no replacement for reading the whole novel, and one or two poems can merely suggest the breadth of expression of which a poet may be capable.

On the other hand, this anthology was intentionally designed as a small collection which could easily fit into the syllabi of history, sociology, or political science courses. In this way, the book can provide a vivid and imaginative accompaniment to standard textbooks.

The Vietnam War was, is, and undoubtedly will remain a complicated, controversial issue. No one writer can claim to fully make sense of this war, but through the multiplicity of views afforded by a fictional approach, the novelist and the poet can offer many possible interpretations of the experience. These interpretations are most valuable if they are carefully considered, analyzed, and discussed. As this collection is intended for use as a teaching instrument, discussion questions are included to guide those still learning how to read complex literature and appreciate all of its potential. In addition, a brief time line will provide basic reference points, a glossary of terms will give the non-veteran access to the unique lexicon of the Vietnam experience, and a brief bibliography will suggest further readings in fiction, poetry and drama.

For their generosity and enthusiasm I would like to thank all the writers who contributed to this collection, especially John Del Vecchio, for his lengthy answers to my many questions about this literature, and Bill Ehrhart, whose advice and help have been invaluable. I would also like to thank my students for their candid responses to the fiction and poetry they read. Finally, I would like to express special thanks to my family for their encouragement and occasional editorial services and above all, to Terry Wilson for his ideas on the style and content of this book and his sincere support of its development.

Introduction

All wars change society. With an average of twenty wars occurring in the world at any given time, cultures, economics, and governments constantly feel the indelible imprint war leaves on the people and nations it touches. Society must come to terms with the changes war brings, but often historical perspectives and popular political ideologies limit attempts to evaluate the impact of war.

Inherent in fiction, however, is a flexibility which can accommodate ambiguity, differing viewpoints, history, philosophy and psychology. Thus many readers believe that literature offers the best way to contemplate war. The poet's images, the novelist's characters, and the playwright's speeches often depict war in a way that is more real than an account of military tactics or peace settlements.

From the writer's point of view, war is rich material. War strips men and women of customary social restraints, places them in extreme situations, and gives them a new moral code. Taken from the security of home and family, the young soldier—whose biggest problem heretofore may have been how to save enough money to buy a Chevy or how to get sweet Sally in the back seat of one—is suddenly thrust into a world where his day to day existence revolves around sophisticated weaponry, military regimentation, and, quite possibly, an environment and climate totally alien to him. Basic training stripped the boy of his identity, making him a hairless, olive drab clone of all the other recruits and new enlistees. Instead of independence and individuality, teamwork and obedience become essential for survival. On top of it all, eighteen or twenty years of being told "Thou shall not kill" is now replaced by "Kill them fuckers, before they kill you!" What more fertile soil could an author ask for in which to plant the seeds of character development, plot, and incisive symbolism?

The proximity of death in a war zone intensifies emotions and highlights acts of courage, cowardice and compassion. Along with the release of society's restraint on aggression, war releases men's ability to express love and tenderness toward each other. The fiction writer can tell us what fear feels like when it is so intense every muscle strains inward and the mind closes to a pinprick of hope. The poet can capture an image of love in two hands held by one, waiting for a Medivac helicopter. No political treatise tells that side of war.

One other reason for studying war literature is that the soldier at war serves as a metaphor for the individual in society. In dealing with overwhelming bureaucracy, working with complex technology, and trying to understand a world of contradictory motives, the soldier's experience is similar to that of modern men and women. The tragic vision of most contemporary writers is easily depicted in a soldier's story— destiny can't be controlled and fate is arbitrary, at best.

In many ways, all wars are alike, and the saying "war is war" is generally true. For the infantryman huddled in a trench or marching through the mud, one war looks much like any other war. Men and women die in all wars; many are wounded, physically and psychologically. All wars have deserters, soldiers missing in action, resentment towards leaders, acts of bravery, fear and frustration. The political and sociological motives for war are always complex and are rarely understood by the average soldier, sailor, mechanic or cook. Civilians suffer and die in all wars. Lands and towns are scarred, and each and every person who is involved in a war will have a different story to tell.

In many ways, all war literature is alike, too. American war literature has established itself through works such as Stephen Crane's *The Red Badge of Courage* (Civil War), Ernest Hemingway's *A Farewell to Arms* (WW I), and Norman Mailer's *The Naked and the Dead* (WW II). These novels share themes and techniques that, by their similarity, reinforce the notion that all wars are alike. Camaraderie, superstition, and the simple mortality of flesh are concepts found in most war literature. Furthermore, the enemy as human, the inability to control time, and the indifference of nature also all appear in most war stories and poems. Women are either idealized or depicted as prostitutes, victimized by the war. Death is irrational, and war is ultimately revealed as vastly different from the myths of Ulysees, King Arthur, and John Wayne. The fact that these similarities exist among war novels and poems should not negate the value of the literature, however. Instead, it should reinforce the idea that in many ways all wars are alike and the warning against war that our writers are trying to issue remains constant.

In many specific ways, though, the Vietnam War was different from other wars Americans fought in. This was the first war where there was extensive anti-war protesting going on at home, some of which, significantly, was by men and women who had previously fought in that war. Public exposure to the war was greater than ever before due to extensive media coverage. Also, the average age of the soldiers was much younger than in World War II: 19 as opposed to 25.8. And, for

America, the Vietnam War was fought primarily by the lower classes due to heavy recruitment in lower income areas. The upper classes had either the money or the college deferment to avoid the draft until the lottery was instated.

For the first time, the term of active duty "in-country" was regulated to 365 days, resulting in the "short-timer's" mentality—counting down the days, seeing little continuity of operation or platoon. There were no mass arrival and indoctrination, no welcome or debriefing upon return. Furthermore, towards the end of the war, drugs became plentiful, as language and moral attitudes at home changed dramatically.

Another difference between the Vietnam War and other wars the United States fought was the body count system. With no fixed goals for winning, such as the taking of ground or liberation of a city, the lines of combat were often blurred. Merely counting dead bodies, presumably the enemy, became the measurement for victory. Obviously this measurement had a great deal of room for error and adjustment.

Perhaps the most significant way the Vietnam War differed for Americans was that we left without a decisive victory. In all previous wars, the United States achieved most of its objectives and emerged strong in national pride and commitment. Some experts say the military lost the war; others say it was the politicians' fault. Still other analysts claim we never had a chance against jungle guerrillas. However it is determined, the result is the same. For the first time, Americans were forced to question the morality of their motives and examine the roots of the patriotism they'd taken for granted for so long.

The literature of this confusing, shattering war must cover many things. It must record the reactions of different types of personalities to the unique experience of this war and determine the amount of responsibility each individual conscience should assume. It must examine the complexities of guerrilla warfare and come to terms with the influence the culture and environment had on the outcome of the war. The role of the media must be analyzed, as well as the discrepancy between Americans' preconceived notions of war and the reality of this one. And finally, this literature should seek an understanding of the change in the national character brought about by our involvement in Vietnam.

Literature is constantly evolving, and the subgenre of American war literature is no exception. Perhaps the most noticeable indicator of this is language. We no longer put dashes in the middle of offensive words, nor do we distort them with phonetic spellings. While not indulged in, shocking graphic descriptions are not avoided to spare the delicate reader. The American literature of the Vietnam War is vibrant, forceful, and often raw. The words spoken by fictional characters and used to create the images of Vietnam are, by necessity, by reality, strong and vivid. We can never learn about this war or any war if we shut our eyes to the horror and open them only for the valor. This literature offers us both, honestly, creatively and in a true spirit of hope and caring.

Novels

Between 1960 and 1970 relatively few novels focusing on the Vietnam War were published. Today, there are hundreds published and more being written. Obviously, the question that is frequently asked is why so few novels appeared before the early 1980s. The answer is threefold.

First of all, time was needed to distance ourselves from the war. Books were being written, but publishers were rejecting them. The wounds were too raw, and reading about a controversial war seemed to be no way to help the country reunite itself politically and socially. Besides, publishing is a business and unpopular topics don't sell. Eight to ten years later, as the war became "history," the public was ready to take another look. The pro-war and anti-war rhetoric of the 1960s was gone, along with some of the sense of guilt, anger and defeat that prevailed after the fall of Saigon. The time that had passed allowed for a more balanced view of the war and a desire to understand the mistakes that were made there. In the early 1980s, then, America was not only ready to read about the war, we were eager to read about it. We finally recognized the need to celebrate the Vietnam War veteran, and the need to acknowledge, truthfully, what happened in Southeast Asia.

The second reason for the time lapse before many Vietnam War novels were published is simply a matter of quality. Good writing takes time. Also, many of these books were first novels; the authors were young and hadn't fully developed their writing skills. It is for this reason too, that several proposed novels either became personal narratives or read like memoirs. Autobiography is less complicated to write than fiction. But, as the many excellent novels of this war demonstrate, if the talent was there and the time was taken, brilliant fiction could be produced.

Patriotism is the third reason so many novels appeared in the 1980s. The United States bounced back from the trauma of the Vietnam War with a vibrant resurgence of patriotism. A robust faith in American echoes throughout the films, music, corporate identities, and political speeches of the eighties, paying tribute to the country—the good moments and the bad.

There is a danger, though, of rewriting history and diminishing the tragedy of the Vietnam War (or any war, for that matter), but the fear of a similar conflict occurring in Central America or the Middle East is also great. Therefore, writers, scholars, politicians and students look for the literature to be accurate. First and foremost, the novels of the Vietnam War tell us to not forget, to remember exactly what the war was like.

The ability to show What This War Was Like is the greatest achievement of the Vietnam War novels. Through penetrating sensory images and precise details, readers are quickly emersed in the confusion, frustration, fear and excitement of Vietnam. Some Vietnam War novels show the war as a manifestation of pure insanity. Others show the conflict as the result of misguided political and strategic theories. Still others present the war as the result of nature being driven out of balance or the clash between Eastern and Western thought. Whatever route a novelist takes towards understanding, the road is always described the same way and that description leaves a powerful impression on the reader.

Furthermore, the effect of Vietnam on contemporary literature doesn't stop with the war novels. Much current fiction shudders with the same sense of alienation and dislocation as the war novels. Authors such as Jayne Anne Phillips, Raymond Carver and Robert Stone resist analyzing their characters' motives, choosing to create a world of disjointed moments which can only be assimilated with the proper amount of detachment and cynicism. The settings may be contemporary America, but the explanations for the characters' behavior begin with Vietnam.

Literary critics and scholars often look for "the novel" of a particular generation, event or location. "The novel" must epitomize the attitudes, actions, and emotions of a situation, as well as be a consummate piece of literature. Unfortunately, "the novel" can't ever exist. Ask any twenty English, history or political science teachers what was "the novel" of World War II, and each one will give a different answer. Stylistic preference and political viewpoints are too subjective.

Even so, readers seem to enjoy arguing whether or not "the novel" of the Vietnam War has been written. The narrowness of veterans' introspection, journalists' dependence on their craft and non-veteran's lack of experience are all offered as arguments against one book or another as "the novel". Still others argue that the media influenced the country's view of the war to such an extent that we couldn't recognize the truth if we saw it; we are either too familiar with the war or too desensitized to it. All these arguments serve little purpose. The novels of the Vietnam War speak in the language of the war, they let us know what it was like, and, in their bildungsroman formats they present an appropriate metaphor for America's loss of innocence. If readers must have "the novel" of this war, let them look again. Many well-qualified candidates are available, many more are on the way.

David Halberstam
One Very Hot Day
1967

Born in 1934, David Halberstam was a reporter for The New York Times *in 1962 when he covered the growing conflict in Vietnam. His reporting won him a Pulitzer Prize in 1964, and he has gone on to write many successful books such as* The Making of Quagmire, The Best and the Brightest, Ho, *and* The Reckoning, *all of which blend his skills as a researcher, reporter and writer.*

In the afterword to One Very Hot Day, *Halberstam writes, "I wanted to portray the frustrations, and the emptiness of this war. It was after all a smaller and, I think, less tidy war than Americans were accustomed to, and almost nothing that happened in it fit the preconceptions of Westerners. So, starting in 1966, I sat down and wrote* One Very Hot Day."

With great immediacy and realism, this novel tells the story of 38-year-old Captain Beaupre, an American advisor to a Vietnamese infantry company. The book focuses on the sense of despair Beaupre feels in his frustrating position. This excerpt shows the absurd bureaucratic fumbling that could easily foul up a typical patrol and Beaupre's inability to do anything about it.

Ap Than Thoi was missing the village: they had missed it six weeks ago on an operation and since then it had become a legendary place. It had been a search and clear operation and they had been warned that the local population might be unfriendly, which, in the particular understatement of the times, meant that they were likely to be very hostile. They made their first stop as scheduled with a minimal amount of success and difficulty, and then they had moved toward their next objective which was Ap Than Thoi, four kilometers away, and reputed to be most unfriendly. They had gone the four kilometers, and they had not found it, and they had gone a little further, another click and a half and they had not found it, and by then the Colonel was on their radio demanding to know if they were in Ap Than Thoi, and if not, why the hell not. A few minutes later he was back on the radio wondering aloud why they were behind schedule, saying that it was goddamned embarrassing at headquarters, embarrassing to the entire American Army, but more important, embarrassing to him, in front of his Asian allies. Beaupre, he said, his voice becoming very correct, was making him look silly in front of Colonel Co, and the Colonel *did not like to look foolish in front of anyone, particularly his Asian counterpart.* It's embarrassing here too, Beaupre had said, and Dang is just as embarrassed as I am. Don't tell me about Dang, the Colonel said, I don't want to hear about your problems, get those ffing Viets off their asses, that's your job. You're not paid to be embarrassed. You're paid to move.

Ten minutes later when they still hadn't reported in from Ap Than Thoi (by this time Beaupre had convinced Dang to send patrols out in all four directions, looking for Ap Than Thoi, and Dang had compiled surprisingly easily, apparently Co was chewing his ass too over the failure to find the village which was making Co lose face at the CP), the Colonel came back on shouting angrily that if they didn't get there, he would come in to Ap Than Thoi himself, by helicopter, he would by God welcome them there and be the goddamn hospitality committee; he would lead their goddamn parade for them and he would carry out on that same ffing helicopter Beaupre's weather-eaten ass, and that shiny new West Point ass too, Anderson's ass, he said a moment later, having forgotten the Lieutenant's name in his excitement. That was when Beaupre had gotten angry. "My weather-eaten ass is now resting at," and then read his coordinates for Ap Than Thoi. The Colonel read them back and they were the same. Beaupre then was angry and excused himself to the Colonel, begging his pardon sir, and announced that they were there, but the village was not. It was the village's fault. He also referred to it as "your Ap Than Thoi."

He sensed from the voice that the Colonel had taken it relatively well; he had read coordinates out, where they were, where they had been, where they were going, and finally again demanded to know where the village was.

"Beg your pardon, sir," Beaupre said, "but there are two Americans and one hundred and fifty Vietnamese wondering the same thing."

"The other side of the canal," the Colonel said, "that's it, the other side of the canal. The map made a mistake."

"Beg your pardon, sir," Beaupre said, "but the map did make a mistake, but it's not the other side of the canal. We've been working it for the last twenty minutes and they don't have it either."

"But there must be a village there, must be people there. Why we even have reports saying the people are hostile, so that proves it. If they're hostile, they've got to be there," the Colonel insisted. "Look around yourself, Captain Beaupre, what do you see?"

"Sir, Vietnamese, a lot of them, a lot of trees, some bushes."

"What are the troops doing, Beaupre?"

"Sir, the troops are sitting down, and talking and some of them are already impurifying the canal, and a few of them are starting to break out the rice."

"Just a minute," the Colonel said. "You wait there a minute, Beaupre, and don't go anywhere. Don't leave the place you're at. Think of it as Ap Than Thoi."

Then he sent a spotter plane over and it circled the area for a few minutes without finding the village or drawing fire. Finally the plane radioed back and the Colonel called Beaupre and said, "Beaupre, cross Ap Than Thoi off your map. Forget about it. It's not your fault, Captain."

Beaupre thanked him (he liked the Colonel) and made a note that someone should draw up some new maps, since these were twenty years old and not always accurate.

That night the Colonel said nothing, but apparently the entire advisory group knew what had happened and almost overnight Ap Than Thoi became a part of the vocabulary. One went away to Saigon but claimed he was going to Ap Than Thoi; someone violently ill for three days claimed he had contracted the bug at Ap Than Thoi; if an officer with a girl met a buddy in Saigon, he always introduced her as being from Ap Than Thoi; if something went wrong in the field, a terrible snafu, it always took place at Ap Than Thoi; if an operation were being planned and someone wanted to know the local political climate, he would be told it was no worse than Ap Than Thoi.

Robert Stone
Dog Soldiers
1973

Robert Stone, who was born in 1937, won the William Faulkner Award in 1968 for Hall of Mirrors *and the National Book Award in 1975 for* Dog Soldiers. *Also to his credit are* A Flag for Sunrise, Children of Light, *and the screenplays for* WUSA *and* Who'll Stop the Rain.

Dog Soldiers *revolves around losers who are driven by greed, fear, boredom and violence. The war in Vietnam is shown as having severely damaged the few crumbling remains of integrity the American conscience may have had.*

With the air conditioner's buzz obliterating the noise from the Saigon street below his hotel room, John Converse rationalizes his way up to and through the immoral implications of smuggling heroin into the United States.

There were moral objections to children being blown out of sleep to death on a filthy street. And to their being burned to death by jellied petroleum. There were moral objections to house lizards being senselessly butchered by madmen. And moral objections to people spending their lives shooting scag.

He stood facing the wall where the lizard stains were, rubbing the back of his neck.

Everyone felt these things. Everyone must, or the value of human life would decline. It was important that the value of human life not decline.

Converse had once accompanied Ian Percy to a color film made by the U. N. soil conservation people about the eradication of termites. In a country that looked something like Nam, where there was elephant grass and red earth and palm trees, the local soldiery drove over the grasslands with bulldozers, destroying immense conical termite colonies. There was a reason, as he remembered; the mounds caused erosion or the termites ate crops or people's houses. The termites were doing something bad. When the colonial mounds were overturned, termites came burrowing up from the ruins in frantic tens of thousands, flourishing their pinchers in futile motions of defense. Soldiers with flame throwers came behind the bulldozers scorching the earth and burning the termites and their eggs to black cinders. Watching the film, one felt something very like a moral objection. But the moral objection was overridden. People were more important than termites.

So moral objections were sometimes overridden by larger more profound concerns. One had to take the long view. It was also true that at a certain point the view might become too long and moral objections appear irrelevant. To view things at such length was an error. The human reference point must be maintained.

Really, Converse thought, I know all about this. He pressed his thumb against the wall and removed a dry particle of reptile spine from its cool surface. It was an error to take the long view in the face of moral objections. And it was an error to insist on moral objections when they were overridden. If one is well grounded in youth, the object of love and sound toilet training, these things became second nature.

In the red field, when the fragmentation bombs were falling out of what appeared to be a perfectly empty blue sky, he had experienced no moral objections at all.

The last moral objection that Converse experienced in the traditional manner had been his reaction to the Great Elephant Zap of the previous year. That winter, the Military Advisory Command, Vietnam, had decided that elephants were enemy agents because the NVA used them to carry things, and there had ensued a scene worthy of the *Ramayana*. Many-armed, hundred-headed MACV had sent forth steel-bodied flying insects to destroy his enemies, the elephants. All over the country, whooping sweating gunners descended from the cloud cover to stampede the herds and mow them down with 7.62-millimeter machine guns.

The Great Elephant Zap had been too much and had disgusted everyone. Even the chopper crews who remembered the day as one of insane exhilaration had been somewhat appalled. There was a feeling that there were limits.

And as for dope, Converse thought, and addicts—if the world is going to contain elephants pursued by flying men, people are just naturally going to want to get high.

So there, Converse thought, that's the way it's done. He had confronted a moral objection and overridden it. He could deal with these matters as well as anyone.

But the vague dissatisfaction remained and it was not loneliness or a moral objection; it was, of course, fear. Fear was extremely important to Converse; morally speaking it was the basis of his life. It was the medium through which he perceived his own soul, the formula through which he could confirm his own existence. I am afraid, Converse reasoned, therefore I am.

Robert Olen Butler
The Alleys of Eden
1981

In 1971 Robert Olen Butler went to Vietnam, first serving in Military Intelligence, then working as an interpreter for the American advisor to the mayor of Saigon. The Alleys of Eden *glows with Butler's understanding of the Vietnamese language and culture. His other novels include* Sun Days, Countrymen of Bones, On Distant Ground, *and most recent,* Wabash. *Butler presently teaches creative writing at McNeese State University in Lake Charles, Louisiana.*

In The Alleys of Eden, *Clifford Wilkes, the last American deserter left in Saigon, is faced with a terrifying decision. He must either join the refugees charging the United States Embassy in hopes of escape to*

*America or remain in Saigon—under seige. Either way, his decision will
also determine the future for Lanh, the Vietnamese woman who has
shared love and shelter with him for nearly five years. Lanh helped him
hide, survive, and come to terms with his acts of war and act of desertion.*

He remembered telling her the story of the killing. He told her late
in the afternoon of their fourth day together, after a long nap, entwined
naked on this bed through the worst heat of the day.

—Can't you think of anything else to confess to me? She mocked.

—I just want you to know what you're getting into.

—And you? Shall I tell you all the things I've been paid to do?

Cliff could not tell if she was serious about this or still mocking
him.

—You don't have anything to confess to me, he said.

—Or the things I did for free? How about those? She was clearly
angry now.

—I'm sorry. It was me I was talking about. Not you. You know
I love you for what you are.

—And can't I do the same? She was gentle now. You helped kill
a man, she said. What did you expect when you came to Vietnam?

Cliff flinched at this and Lanh drew him close. Cut it out, she said.
Listen to me. That man expected the same thing. He was more ready
than you. Why was he so quiet when he knew he was going to die?

—He was afraid.

—No. Not just that. He was quiet because he is Vietnamese and
he knew that dying like that was part of life. As natural as he can squat
and take rice under a banyan tree and bury his daddy in the fields and
bury a burned child, he can die from the way things are in this country.
It was the way of your job here. It was part of his way too. He knew
and accepted that. So he didn't speak when the water that had grown
his rice squeezed at his heart. We're all alike in this place. We understand
you see.

Cliff pulled away from Lanh. He had to see her eyes at this. She
was looking at him calmly. With love, even. He could not even begin
to fully understand what feelings lay behind her words. But he did know
the look. She touched his face, pressed his eyes shut with her fingertips.

—You forgive me? he asked.

She kissed him on the eyes.

Another moment, much later. He pressed too hard to tell her his
desire for her. You're beautiful, Lanh. So beautiful.

She turned on him sharply. You'd trade me in for the first pair
of size 36 American breasts you could get your hands on, she said.

—No. Not true.

—I don't believe you. You'd be crazy to love a tiny little dark thing like me.

Cliff went deeper in, though he'd learned long ago he should just be quiet at times like this. You call me crazy, he said, because I appreciate you? Then are they sane men who come here to fight a war but find you small and yellowish and similar so they go with ease beyond just war and torture your people?

Even as he spoke of torture he realized how totally Lanh had let him forget what he'd done. The word burred in his mind but Lanh would not take advantage of it in the argument.

—Don't pity me, Cliff, she said. Don't do it. Don't pity the strange little people who need someone with sharp eyes to love them.

—I don't feel that way, Cliff cried.

—And don't talk to me about torture. You expect me to fall weeping now for my persecuted people? Must I weep for them all and never stop weeping?

—No.

—They understand. If I am in our fields and the sun wears me down, I go under a tree and sit quiet, feel warm, take my joy, but the hot sun is all around me. I see it, I know it's part of where I am. If there is no tree, I must sit in the field and accept it.

—We took your trees. We burned them away.

—Why is your coming to us any different from the coming of the heat of the day? You live too. If you don't come, then that is the way of our life. But you did come, and if you kill me slowly, I will feel pain and die. But don't cut me off from the life around me, don't make me die bad, let me keep my acceptance of things.

—You know I've always fought you about your envy of American women. I love you, Lanh. I don't want you to look or think or act or feel like an American.

—Then speak to somebody else about the torture. I can't hear it again.

There was a long pause. Cliff sat on the bed staring at the floor. He hadn't really felt guilty anymore. She'd cleared that out of him long ago. That was the irony. But she was in pain and there was nothing he could do to remove it. Not as she had done for him. She was beside him on the bed. Her voice was gentle.

—We don't need to ever think about those things, she said. Not between us.

Cliff lay down beside her now in the dark room. He pulled the sheet over him and they lay together, side by side on their backs, hands at their sides, as if laid out together in death.

John Del Vecchio
The 13th Valley
1982

Born in 1947, John Del Vecchio was drafted in 1970, a year after he graduated from Lafayette College. In Vietnam he served as combat correspondent in the 101st Airborne Division (Airmobile). Del Vecchio currently lives in Connecticut where he is working on his second novel.

The 13th Valley *is a masterpiece of realistic fiction, giving a resonant account of what it was like to be a boonierat—a typical infantryman— in the jungles of Vietnam. The characters in this novel are powerfully developed and the military movements carefully researched.*

This excerpt, located three fifths of the way through the book, describes one afternoon of the thirteen day operation in which troops from the 101st were sent into the Khe Ta Laou Valley to attack the 7th NVA front headquarters.

It was still raining when the column reached the abrupt face of the north escarpment. They had come 400 meters from the river through elephant grass and bamboo without feeling any apparent elevation change and then they hit the road and the mountain cliff.

"Oh my Holy Mother," Garbageman gasped seeing the road. 2d Plt had led off again after everyone had tightened and tied off clothing against the leech invasion. The point squad had changed from Catt's to Mohnsen's. Garbageman was at point, Smith, with his 60, at slack. Where they hit the road at the base of the mountain there was a ten foot wide all-weather road, not only reinforced with bamboo but solidified with gravel. It was adjacent to the cliff and ran as far as Garbagemen could see in the fog in both directions. Elephant grass formed a cleanly trimmed wall along the valley side of the road, the cliff had been evenly cleaved on the other shoulder. Again, grass and bamboo had been woven into living nets to form a natural-looking roof. From the air the roof would appear to be unbroken jungle valley floor and it would conceal all road traffic. To Garbageman standing in the vegetation ogling the road, it was evident that NVA honchos had established the road here because of the difficulty helicopters would have molesting troop or munitions traffic. Garbageman had never seen an enemy road so wide, wide enough for two-way cart traffic, wide enough for trucks. It made the red balls look like animal trails. The surface was rutted with recent signs of activity yet showed signs of continuous care and maintenance.

Smitty up, Garbageman signaled. Smith came forward. "Go back and get De Barti and Pop," Garbageman whispered. "They gotta check this the fuck out, Man." Word passed back. Pop Randalph came forward, then Lt. De Barti. "L-T gonna have to see this," they agreed and they radioed the CP. The boonierats of the lead squad fanned out in the grass forming a T at the columnhead. The column halted.

Brooks, his three RTOs and FO worked their way to point. From the depths of the grass they all examined the road.

"What do you think, Ruf?" De Barti asked the L-T very quietly. They were separated from the others by six or seven feet. De Barti did not want to expose his deep apprehension to the troops, "I don't think we oughta use it."

Brooks pulled out his topo map without answering and the two lieutenants studied it. "If we can find a way up the cliff..." Brooks began.

"No way we're goin up that shit," De Barti said. "It's vertical."

"It can't be vertical for very far," Brooks said. The two mused over the map and peered out of the grass at the road. They could see only a small strip. Brooks removed his hat and scratched his scalp. Go back through the leeches and recross the river, go up the road, down the road, try to climb the cliff. All about him the boonierats were becoming more and more restless. It was getting near dusk. With a road like this, he thought, the NVA could have thousands of troops in here. Brooks went to Cahalan. "Get me Red Rover," he said. "Bill," he turned to FO, "have you ever come across a road like this?"

"No, L-T, can't say I have."

"Can you get arty on it?"

"Yes Sir. Can do."

"Good. Call in targets all along this contour."

"L-T," Cahalan whispered, "I've got the GreenMan."

The GreenMan was at the forward TOC on Firebase Barnett. For him the day had held several torturous decisions, the most difficult having been whether or not to commit Bravo Company to a full-scale assault against the NVA bunker complex. Rain and fog had socked in the valley and the rear and all helicopter support except emergency medical evacuation had been cancelled. Bravo could retreat and attack tomorrow although they would run the risk of being hit tonight or Bravo could attack without helicopter support. Bravo attacked. When Cahalan reached the GreenMan, Bravo had overrun the bunker complex, killed seventeen enemy soldiers and suffered five wounded. The medevac bird from Eagle Dust-Off, along with the four escort Cobras and a chase ship, a Huey on station to pick up the medevac crew should that helicopter be shot down, was approaching Bravo's location.

"Quiet Rover, this is Red Rover," the GreenMan snarled after Brooks had reported briefly about the enemy road, "proceed to your echo by november echo ASAP. Caution your papa Sky Devil Six is to your november one kilo. Play ball with Sky Devil."

"Who's Sky Devil?" De Barti asked Cahalan.

"Ah, that'd be Delta Company, Sir," Cahalan answered.

"Oh fuck," De Barti groaned. "Not that clusterfuck."

Brooks described the road in greater detail, hoping the GreenMan would be able to assist him. He did not want to have his company march down the enemy road. It appeared impossible to cross the road and ascend the cliffs at that point, yet he felt he had to get off the valley floor. As he conversed on the radio the sound of helicopters above the valley pulsated the wet air.

"Get me a full reconnaissance of that feature," The GreenMan directed. "And, play ball with Sky Devil. Out."

Oh shit, Brooks thought. "Roger that, niner. Wilco. Out". Brooks looked around. He directed Cahalan to establish communication with Delta Company to determine Delta's exact position and to see if the Delta Darlings had found a way up and down the cliff face. "Tell them," Brooks said, "Red Rover wants us to rendezvous. It'll be a hell of a lot better if we can get up to them on the ridge than to have them come down here." Brooks turned to FO again and asked, "Where do you think this road goes?"

"I don't really know," FO said. "Like you figure, it probably follows the contours pretty close. If the dinks are moving heavy material, they'd a built the road as level as possible."

"After we get out of range, have arty seal this thing off behind us. See if they'll drop some rounds west of here right now."

It was 1800 hours when Alpha began moving again. Garbageman was still at point, Smitty and Pop walked a double slack. Slowly, apprehensively, Garbageman stepped onto the road and into the dark corridor formed by the grass wall and the cliff. He scanned up and back. Fog limited visibility to under twenty meters. The pointman turned right and began moving. Carefully he checked the mountain wall which rose to his left. The slacks emerged from the grass eight feet behind point, they split and walked one on each side of the road. Mohnsen and Jones emerged next continuing the double pattern set by the slacks, then Greer and Roberts, Sklar and De Barti, and El Paso and Brooks.

Oh Man, I don't like this one fucken bit, Garbageman whispered to himself. He stopped and crouched. Both slacks moved up and squatted by the point. "This is a Goddamned highway," Garbageman whispered. "Man I don't dig this shit one fucken bit. This don't even make sense."

"Want me to walk point?" Pop asked, his eyes twinkling.

That was the ultimate affront, the most severe attack on the Garbageman's manhood and pride. "Naw," he whispered. "I can do it."   •

"Maybe we oughta both do it," Pop gave him an alternative that he could accept without losing face.

"Ah, yeah," Garbageman seized the chance. They rose and with one at each edge proceeded in double point with a single slack.

2d Plt was followed onto the road by the remainder of the CP. All the RTOs had folded their flexible radio antennas that protruded from their rucks and labeled them as valuable communication targets. El Paso had slid his antenna into his belt, Cahalan stuck his into a hole in his shirt, Brown rolled his in a loop and forced it back down into the ruck. 3d Plt followed the CP and 1st followed 3d. They moved very slowly, very quietly. It took almost half an hour for the entire column to turn the corner from the narrow jungle grass passage onto the enemy supply road. The boonierats continued the double column. They remained on the road, heading east, looking for an opening in the cliff they might ascend up to the ridge. They maintained wide intervals. By the time Silvers, at drag, finally stepped onto the road, Alpha was spread 125 meters long.

Silvers came onto the road behind Brunak. He stood at the intersection for several minutes, staring to the rear, allowing the column to progress away from him. An artillery round burst 700 meters west, the concussion rumbling up the road and echoing in from the south escarpment a fraction of a second apart. Silvers turned and quickly marched to catch up. As he reached a point 30 meters from where he had left the grass he turned to look back. A single explosive pop cracked the air. Silvers dropped in the center of the road. Every man in Alpha dove for cover. There was another crack. Boonierats dove into the grass, scrambled for concealment, searched for a target. Brunak had been hit by the second round. "Bravo, Bravo," a squashed tight-chest scream for a medic escaped from his throat. Boonierats raced through the grass toward him. No one had found a target. No one fired. Marko, Jax and Lairds surrounded Brunak. They expected follow-up fire. None came. Marko aimed his 60 down the road. There was nothing there. He aimed the weapon over Silver's body which had collapsed backward on the rucksack it had been carrying. Silvers' helmet had fallen off and rolled away. His legs had doubled beneath his body before the body had toppled backward and spread across the pack. The head slumped back over the ruck, the eyes stared upside-down motionless down the vacant road upon which Alpha had trespassed.

"Bravo," Jax yelled from beside Brunak.

Egan, Whiteboy and Doc McCarthy came crashing through the grass. Others were coming back. Most had shed their rucks. Brunak screamed. McCarthy squatted by his side. 1st Sqd with Egan and several others maneuvered down through the grass past Silvers and formed a perimeter.

Cherry, Thomaston and Moneski's squad reacted second, rushing back and reinforcing the soldiers about Brunak. Doc Johnson sprinted down the center of the road running like a madman, his aid bag in one hand, a .45 in the other. Doc dove into the mud behind Silvers. He got to his knees and hunched over the body. There was a splat of blood in the center of Silvers' throat. Working quickly yet gently Doc lifted Leon's head. The neck no longer had a back. The bullet had entered through the soft flesh below Silvers' chin then tumbled and ripped its way out the nape of the neck carrying most of the cervical vertebrae, the surrounding muscle tissue, the trachea, esophagus, arteries, veins and a tremendous amount of blood.

In the grass McCarthy worked on Brunak. Brunak had caught a round in the right side. It was difficult to determine how badly he had been hit but McCarthy was sure it was bad. Brunak was laughing, then tensing, cramping his entire body, then laughing again, flowing from consciousness, pain and spasms, to empty shock. McCarthy applied a field dressing to the hole in Brunak's side and jabbed him with a syringe of morphine. From his aid bag he took a 500ml plastic bag labeled Plasma Protein Fraction (Human). The plasma solution came in a kit complete with IV needle and airway cannula. McCarthy pumped Brunak's arm then jammed the needle in. He knew he was missing as soon as the needle broke the skin. He yanked it out. Brunak flinched. Then he laughed. McCarthy stuck him again and began the IV flow.

On the trail Doc Johnson had closed Silvers' eyes. The medic methodically wrapped a large sterile dressing about the dead man's neck so no one would see the extent of the damage. Doc pulled a towel from Silvers' ruck and placed part of it behind Leon's head. He brought the remainder over the sallow face. Then, holding his aid bag, Doc rolled off the trail into the grass.

Cherry squatted in the grass beside Thomaston. He awaited directions. Egan came back to them. He grabbed the handset, radioed El Paso, explained the situation, and requested a priority medevac. He tossed the hook back to Cherry and snapped, "Git down. I don't want ta call in a bird for you too."

Hoover crawled over the group about Brunak. Thomaston grabbed his hook and radioed the CP. "We're moving back into the grass fifty meters," he said after talking to Brooks. "We'll get the Dust-Off out there."

Thomaston and Egan directed the perimeter to move further down while they, with Jax' help, pulled Silvers' body from the road. With the others breaking a trail and then crushing a tiny clearing toward the valley center, Egan and Jax jumped back onto the road and pulled Silvers' body, ruck and weapon into the grass. Jax separated the ruck from the body of his dead field partner. He lifted the body gently and carried it to the clearing. "Yo gowin be alright now, Leon, my friend," Jax whispered smoothingly. "Yo kin relax and fo'get this place." Cherry followed carrying the blood-soaked ruck. Lairds brought the extra weapon and helmet. Brunak, McCarthy and 2d Sqd had already reached and secured the clearing. 3d Plt pulled back to reinforce the evac site, 2d Plt and the CP circled the perimeter in recon patrols, pushing to points 100 meters from the designated pick-up zone.

"Hey," Egan said to Cherry. "You need some good shit?"

"What shit?"

"Here," Egan said rustling through Silvers' equipment. He tossed Cherry a two-quart canteen.

Cherry looked at it, then walked over to the ruck. Across the top, blood drenched but unharmed, was a five-quart water blivet. Cherry untied it. The blivet was a double-layered plastic bladder enclosed in a strong nylon bag, the three bags joined at the top with a canteen neck and screw cap. Water blivets were less cumbersome than canteens and they could be used as pillows. They were in very short supply. "I'd like to take this," Cherry said.

"You got it," Egan answered.

"And his bayonet."

"Take it."

Numbnuts let Cherry and Egan leave the ruck before he went over and scavenged all C-rat meals that were not Ham and Lima Beans. Denhardt scavenged Brunak's ruck.

It was after sunset, late dusk, when the medical evacuation helicopter finally found Alpha. The thick mist prevented the Dust-Off commander from seeing marking smoke and it was not dark enough to use the mini-strobes. The birds even had difficulty finding the valley for all of northern I Corps lay in thick fog and rain. The Dust-Off had first to locate Barnett, then follow a vector path 268 degrees, almost due west.

Cherry directed the bird's approach by ear. "You're passing to our sierra maybe two hundred meters," he called. Then again, "You're approaching us. You're passing over us right, right...now."

The helicopter made a half-dozen passes, at first so high it could not be seen through the fog, then lower and lower. Finally it hovered 15 meters over their position. From the ground Cherry could see the crew chief standing on the left skid and the medic standing on the right. Huge red crosses were painted on white squares on the bird's bottom and sides. The rotor wash from the bird made the rain slam down and sting on upturned faces. Escort ships could be heard circling though they could not be seen. From the right side of the helicopter stuck a three-foot arm and from that dropped a small torpedo-shaped object on a steel cable. The torpedo dropped evenly and in seconds it was on the ground. Doc Johnson, Doc McCarthy, Thomaston and Jax grabbed the torpedo and unfolded it.

"What's that thing?" Cherry questioned.

"Jungle penetrator," Egan answered.

The four men lifted Brunak and his gear and strapped him into a sitting position on the now unfolded, tri-pronged, anchor-like seat. They strapped his gear across from him. Thomaston stretched his arms up over his head and extended his thumbs signaling the crew chief to take him away. The hoist cranked and Brunak rose, swayed beneath the bird, and ascended. The medic reached out and pulled him in. The bird departed, circled and returned. The procedure was repeated with the body and gear of Leon Silvers. Then the medevac departed for good. No trace of the dead or the wounded remained except for blood and neck tissue in the midst of the enemy road and the blood stain on Cherry's water blivet.

Stephen Wright
Meditations in Green
1983

Drafted in 1969, Stephen Wright worked in Military Intelligence in Vietnam through 1970. Afterward, at the University of Iowa, Wright attended the Writer's Workshop, earned an MFA, and taught creative writing. His first novel, Meditations in Green, *won the Maxwell Perkins Prize in 1983.*

Meditations in Green whirls around the character of Spec. 4 James Griffin, an image analyst for the 1069th, who now lives in New York, strung out on heroin, meditating on plants, and racing towards self destruction. Griffin's drug induced flashbacks slowly unveil his story of Vietnam—irrational officers, stoned soldiers, innocence, violence and absurdity. These two brief excerpts exemplify the kaleidoscopic language and clever cynicism of Wright's electrifying novel.

This is not a settled life. A children's breakfast cereal, Crispy Critters, provokes nausea; there is a woman's perfume named Charlie; and the radio sound of "We Gotta Get Out Of This Place" (The Animals, 1965) fills me with a melancholy as petrifying as the metal poured into casts of galloping cavalry, squinting riflemen, proud generals, statues in the park, roosts for pigeons. My left knee throbs before each thunderstorm. The sunsets are no damn good here. There are ghosts on my television set. What are we to do when the darkness comes on and we wait for something to happen, as Huey, who never even knew she shared her name with a ten-thousand-pound assault helicopter, sprawls on the floor with her sketchbook, making pastel pictures of floating cities, sleek spaceships, planets of ice, and I, your genial storyteller, wreathed in a beard of smoke, look into the light and recite strange tales from the war back in the long ago time.

*   *   *

One night a tear gas grenade went off in the O club's air conditioner, sending the assembled leadership hacking, crying, stumbling for the doors.

A deed so popular, the First Sergeant informed Major Holly, that more than five people immediately claimed credit for its success.

One night, the XO claimed, some unknown person or persons took a couple shots at him as he strolled down the officers' walk near the CO's hootch.

Had they mistaken him for me? thought Major Holly.

One morning the First Sergeant, while cutting flowers for the orderly room's daily bouquet, discovered a head in Major Holly's tulip beds. Oriental, male, late teens—early twenties, identity unknown. "Maybe it just growed," suggested the Flight Surgeon. "Get it out of here," ordered Major Holly.

Was that a message for me? he wondered.

One morning, as most of the unit stood in insolent attitudes of at-ease listening to the First Sergeant's monthly medical lecture on the horrors of the Black Syph, Uncle Sam, the unit's Vietnamese carpenter, a hammer dangling from his web belt, castoff combat boots curled up at the toes like a genie's slippers, and his tool-box-toting crew crossed the dirt road before the tracking eyes of the entire formation and entered the orderly room. In a few minutes the morning calm was shattered by the sudden comical sounds of outrageous banging and sawing. The First Sergeant visualized the venereal enemy for them as a thousand-legged, hairy-bodied, sewer-colored bug with honed pincers and razor teeth that loved nothing better than dining out on nerve ends and soft tasty brain matter. After a while the noise stopped, an empty truck pulled up, and Uncle Sam and his crew began carting out of the orderly room basket after basket of fresh dirt. The First Sergeant advised everyone to check their underwear regularly and if it ever looked like someone had blown their nose in there it was time to visit the dispensary.

By noon the whole 1069th knew.

"It's a tunnel," reported Simon, "from the orderly room to his hootch, from his hootch to the command bunker. We'll probably never see him again."

And outside of the occasional office glimpse no one ever did. Their commanding officer had gone underground.

Jeff Danziger
Lieutenant Kit
1986

Jeff Danziger served in Vietnam in 1969-1970 as an intelligence officer and interpreter in the 1st Air Cavalry. He is currently a political cartoonist with The Christian Science Monitor.

The title character of Lieutenant Kit *is an innocent: a handsome young soldier who seems to be oblivious to the absurdity and danger of the war around him. Kit also appears to be completely incompetent, but he draws affection and admiration for his apparent immunity to the war's corruption. In this excerpt, with understated, cynical humor Danziger establishes the character of Major Bedford, one of Kit's superiors.*

In 1971, when the war had become not a war but a disaster, Kit lived in a bunker on the west side of a muddy smelly field with some other lieutenants. Major Bedford, an unhappy, overweight man who thought Kit was a fool, lived in a bunker on the other side.

From the outside, Major Bedford's bunker looked just as damp, cramped, inhospitable and unsanitary as any of the others, but inside there were improvements provided by the inhabitants to honor their higher ranks. Major Bedford's room, for example, had a small Japanese refrigerator and an electric coffee pot.

Major Bedford had talked the other officers in the bunkers, who were for the most part majors like himself, into assigning a small room in a corner of the building to their houseboy, Thi Tuan, so he could stay overnight. It was a violation of the rules, but Thi Tuan was a pleasant young man, and it was handy to have someone in the bunker all night. And during the day Thi Tuan did provide some protection against revenge visits from their own enlisted men, seeking to redress some fancied injustice.

Thi Tuan was also effective against the rats in the bunker. He had invented a tilting box trap which was ingeniously simple, and which Major Bedford was sure would have made Thi Tuan a rich man in a more highly developed economy. After the rat was caught, Thi Tuan pounded it to death with a length of steel pipe and then threw the corpse into the drainage ditch. He could have been even more effective if they had allowed him some ammunition, but that was also against the rules, rules with which they agreed.

Thi Tuan liked Major Bedford, and he paid special decorative attention to Major Bedford's room. He painted the walls red. Over Major Bedford's tiny desk he wired up a display of the arms and military paraphenalia. Two Chinese rifles, which Major Bedford had secretly bought from some infantry soldiers to bring home as war trophies, were crossed. A bandolier of rifle magazines draped from one butt to the other. Above this display was a picture of Major Bedford's wife, an American flag and a picture of William C. Westmoreland cut from *Time* magazine. To Thi Tuan's mind this was the essence of the victory to come—Chinese arms contradicted by a swashbuckling bravery under the aegis of Old Glory and two prominent jaws. Major Bedford realized that his room looked ridiculous, but he felt a morose fatherly affection for Thi Tuan.

He paid Thi Tuan to re-starch and re-press his fatigues when they came back from the village laundry, with careful attention to the creases on the upper arms and the collar. Thi Tuan, using a piece of plywood stored under the bed and an iron brought from the States and spray starch bought in the PX, rendered them as crisp and crackling as if they had come from the most proficient stateside laundry. And no matter how gloomy he felt, Major Bedford could dress with some confidence every morning, cross the muddy field in back of the mess hall, stepping carefully on the rickety boardwalk, walk through the squalid disarray of the transport compound, by the barb-wire confusion of the main gate, down the claymore flanked division street and show up at the headquarters briefing room looking as precise and military as anyone this side of the Pacific.

If he had not been as ready to excuse Major Bedford's behavior as he was, Thi Tuan might have thought him a vain man which would have been a cruel misjudgement. In fact such a misjudgement would have been possible only by someone unfamiliar with the career realities of the American military. And in these realities, Major Bedford had schooled himself with the concentration of a sailor studying the escape hatches when his ship is sinking. For Major Bedford's army career was, if not yet sinking, at best dead in the water.

It had been a sobering day when he finally made the rank of major. He had been promoted after being passed over twice, and in the army scheme of things, the third chance is the last chance. A year before, when he had finally made the promotion list, he had breathed a short sigh of relief, cut short by the immediate realization that, unless there were a marked slaughter of lieutenant colonels, this was to be his last promotion.

The army had subtle ways of communicating its intentions. A begrudged promotion, given only because of a shortage of officers, was scarcely a promotion at all. Your presence is not desired, but under the circumstances, required. The rank is conferred, but don't get used to it.

Of course, it was still very possible that the war would get worse—it certainly wasn't getting any better—and he had read enough history to have faith in politicians to act on his behalf. But still, he was miserable.

He had nowhere else to go. He had too many years in the army to retreat without a fight. If he were not to fight for his country, he would certainly fight for himself, and he wondered if the army ever realized how dedicated an adversary they created in a man with nowhere else to go.

He had developed the most curious attitude toward his rank—he was neither proud of it nor ashamed. He felt it was essentially nothing, comparable to an assistant principal or something in a suburban school. The rank of major was the hardest to bear of all ranks since no one, not those above, nor those below, and certainly not those of equal rank were impressed. No one ever made the claim that they were a major-retired, except maybe Major Hoople. It was too shameful.

With so little promise, some men would have had trouble rising each morning. But Major Bedford managed it somehow. He was awakened regularly by a small bell which hung over his bed which Thi Tuan rang by means of a string which ran out to the narrow hall through a hole in the wall. Thi Tuan would keep ringing until Major Bedford woke and had grunted his permission to stop.

He usually tried to avoid contemplation of his problems early in the morning, but one morning, he had woken in such a state of damp sadness, that he indulged himself in a full review and planning session as he sat on the side of his bed and waited for the blood to equalize itself throughout his body. He sat for some minutes in the gloomy light that filtered through the cracks in the wall, then switched on the overhead light. His clock said three. Even though the generator had gone down in the night he was on time, thanks to the reliability of Thi Tuan, which was in turn the reliability of himself. The fan circulated the heavy morning air over his solid shape.

His shaving mirror was too small to reflect the entire expanse of his face, but what he could see was enough to confirm his belief that no miracles had taken place overnight, further confirmation that they never would. It was a face of much flesh, of virtually no sharp angles, no dramatic chiseled planes, no clefts, no overhangs or promontories, not even clearly defined jowls. The lower line of his face was a firm round arc with a slightly protruding chin. His cheeks were round and soft with a healthy glow nearly as red as a birthmark. His permanent boyish flush would not go away and gave him, as he feared, a clownish appearance.

His eyes were dark, but too narrow. When he made the slightest attempt at some of the expressions necessary for a commanding officer— such as the questioning arch of the eyebrows, the discerning squint, the sarcastic quizzical grin, the accusatory fleer, the longsuffering stare into the middle distance—any of these made his eyes into oriental slits.

In plainer, more painful terms, he did not have a military face, and to be consistent, he did not have a military body. His shoulders, although massive did not taper to a narrow waist; the trunk of his body was thick and despite heroic bouts of dieting, his stomach would not recede. The fullness of the jungle fatigues did conceal his shape to some extent, but he had noticed that even in this outpost of civilization, where nightly mortar attacks were common, where he had very nearly been killed by a rocket two days ago, even here where they lived in the midst of mud and garbage and rats, even here in the most decadent phase of the war, the staff officers were beginning to have their fatigues tailored. If this practice became fashionable, he would have the same problem he had had back in the states—the revelation, through tailoring, of the un-Westmorelandlike thickness of his body.

In the army outward appearances were as important and as unfair as they were anywhere else in life. The military ethic called for spare, stark and certainly untailored accoutrements. Out on the firebases, the officers were as uncouth and dirt-caked as the men, but at the headquarters the tailored staff officers looked patently effeminate. This comparison shocked Major Bedford, and he wondered why no one else mentioned it.

He could take advantage of neither motif. He could not have his fatigues cut tighter because he would reveal his sagging physique. And he could not affect the sloppy dusty insouciance of the field because he was only the civil affairs officer, and one could not get very dusty, and certainly not very insouciant, while distributing rice and corrugated roofing to the villagers. In his solid, round-faced, slow-moving way he looked like the very thing he must, at all costs, not look like. He looked like the thing most diametrically opposed to a commanding officer.

He looked like a sergeant.

This was a particular appearance which career sergeants, after years of drinking mess hall coffee and eating mess hall food, years of tolerating orderly room boredom, years of swilling beer at fetid NCO clubs, took on and maintained with more coffee, heavy food and beer. They were distinguishable from all angles, even from above. Major Bedford knew that his resemblance to a career sergeant was his greatest obstacle, and probably insurmountable.

This physical block was unfair and maddening. What difference did it make what he looked like so long as he was good at his job? Never mind. What difference, the question really was, did it make if it were fair so long as it was?

There was some hope. There was, in his face, the slightest hint of worldly disillusion, of foreboding wisdom and mordancy. No one could know that his expression was caused by self-centered contemplation of topics as unimportant as his own career, and they might just interpret his gloom as the outward manifestation of a world-weary soul and an overburdened memory within. It was possible that his mood and manner would project what his physical appearance could not. If he practiced certain expressions and grimaces, if he affected a philosophoical, saturnine attitude, it might be reasoned by others that within lay a soul so broadened and deepened by the experience of war that its owner was destined to come forward to command where shallower individuals, regardless of their angular physiques, had failed.

It was a subtle point, barely noticeable, barely enough on which to pin his hopes. Major Bedford had no doubts about the way the army made up its mind. It was not known to be sensitive to subtle points.

He knew the army. The only way you could get it to do what you wanted was to force it into a corner and give it no other choice. It would be advisable to have some visible sign to go along with this subtleness, something more glaring to flag him as a man of maturity and wisdom who had seen the dirty side of war. He needed something to show that he had seen the dirty side, because the truth was he hadn't.

Perhaps a wound. A Purple Heart.

How could he go about getting a wound? A visible sign of all that he had supposedly been through, which, together with a limp or facial scar, would announce that there was a soldier with a history. Here was not just an overweight major in a dead-end career.

Getting wounded was not an easy a thing to do, even in the middle of a war zone. Accidental injury was all around, and there were stray projectiles in the air most of the time. But he must do this with some consideration for what the result would be. It had to be the right sort of wound. The Purple Heart was only awarded for those wounded in the course of some sort of hostile enemy action, but he wasn't sure exactly what the regulations said. Besides he couldn't have just any sort of wound. Shot in the foot for example, he might attract nicknames like "leadfoot"; shot on the rear, "leadbottom"; a groin injury might be displeasing even to think about, and then presumably nobody *would* think about it. A belly wound had an ugly painfulness about it, and the less attention drawn to his stomach line the better.

He settled on an injury to the arm or leg, one of the places where people who wrote movies always wounded their heroes, or people they intended to use later in the plot. He reached down and stroked the thick round muscle of his calf. Even here there was no angularity. He would not only have to make plans for how to injure himself, but he would have to do it in the middle of an attack in order to qualify for a medal.

Why was it so hard to get properly and safely wounded in a war? Even that handsome useless fool, Lieutenant Kit, had not managed to do himself enough injury when presented with a perfect opportunity. Kit had been in a jeep that overturned when the driver panicked in the middle of a mortar attack. The enlisted men in the jeep had been seriously hurt. But Kit had somehow rolled clear and had not received a scratch. He hadn't had the presence of mind to cut himself on something.

Major Bedford knew what he would have done, or at least he thought he knew. But sitting here with the solid soft white mass of living muscle in his hand, he began to wonder. Could he cut himself with or on a jagged piece of steel, not just a little scratch, but a real gash? Could he force himself to puncture himself, spurred on by the knowledge that it was a necessary career move, and comforted by the thought that he was only minutes from some of the best medical treatment ever provided by a nation to the brave men who defended its interests? Could he do such a thing?

He could imagine himself in a mortar attack, the usual confusion, with dirt and pieces of buildings flying around, himself running for cover, spotting a jagged edge of steel runway planking. He would run toward it. He would trip.

The injury would be over in a minute, the flesh parted and the bone exposed, hopefully. But could he do it? This act of throwing oneself against sharp steel would require not the abandon he had originally supposed, but an incalculable amount of self-control. He would have to control the involuntary lurch away from his purpose, let his body fall toward the steel, give fate its direction and let it take him where it would. It would require exactly what the citations for bravery always said—a complete disregard for his own personal safety. The old bromides were true—it was not until the battle started and the shells began to fly that a man new the strength of his own spirit and the depth of his own soul.

God! He was going mad.

Of course the best would be a facial wound. There was something notably military about a facial scar.

He took the mirror again and held it before his face. Then with his other hand he squeezed the red flesh of his cheek so that a deep crease ran vertically from just below his right eye to his jaw. He squeezed hard for ten seconds and released the flesh. For a few seconds a white track blazed across his cheek, disturbing the rosy symmetry, and down the middle of this mock scar tissue ran a dark red line. What could have done this? A piece of shrapnel? A bayonet?

Then the blood rushed back in, pumped by his healthy and well-nourished heart. For a quarter of a minute he had been wiser, sadder and stronger, a man who had not only seen the enemy but had faced him. Now the effect was gone, and in its place was the fleshy face of a man whose best attribute probably was his reliable averageness.

He put his mirror down.

He had done enough thinking for this morning. He knew that he had come as close to real madness as he dared. So far it was a controlled madness. Perhaps if he let himself go completely he would be visited by the kind of genius which usually accompanies madness. Could a man bring on madness by the willful act of summoning it? Were there drugs that would help?

Worse than the fact that his thinking this morning had produced no useable conclusions was the sad realization that he was suddenly extremely hungry, and there was no time for breakfast.

He got off the bed and put on his robe and shower shoes. He barely had time to shower and shave and still be in time for the morning briefing. He picked up his razor and towel and stepped out into the narrow hall.

As he walked to the shower, he looked across the mud field and caught sight of Lieutenant Kit leaving hurriedly for the briefing. He was tall and slim and handsome, but at the same time he had a ridiculous, awkward gait that was unmistakable.

For some reason Kit was wearing a helmet although no mortar attacks ever took place in the morning. Major Bedford wondered if some new intelligence had been received that indicated mortar attacks in the morning.

He went through his entire shower with this nagging fear in his mind, when in fact Lieutenant Kit was wearing his helmet only because, as often happened, he couldn't find his hat.

Study Questions

1. What kind of man is Beaupre in Halberstam's *One Very Hot Day?* How does he respond to his superiors, his men, and the situation?

2. How is a sense of absurdity established in *One Very Hot Day* and Wright's *Meditations in Green?*

3. Analyze the way John Converse progresses through his rationalization in the excerpt from Stone's *Dog Soldiers.*

4. Analyze Lanh's attitude to death and the war, as shown in the excerpt from Butler's *The Alleys of Eden.*

5. Why does Butler describe Cliff and Lanh "as if laid out together in death"?

6. *The 13th Valley* is said to give the reader a true sense of what the war, Vietnam, the soldiers, and the jungle were like. Discuss how this realism is created in Del Vecchio's work. Consider the description of the surroundings, the way the men talk, and the action.

7. Discuss the soldiers' response to Silvers' death in *The 13th Valley.*

8. Discuss the comic elements in Wright's *Meditations in Green* and Danziger's *Lieutenant Kit.*

9. What are the many ironies evident in the first paragraph excerpted from *Meditations in Green?*

10. In *Lieutenant Kit,* what is Major Bedford's worst problem, if one could be designated?

Short Stories

While novels slowly unveil complex, intertwined plots with meticulous character portraits, short stories are streamlined, aiming at a single, unified effect. One plot, carefully arranged to hold the reader's interest and arouse suspense, will provide the framework. The characters must be established quickly, so the conflicts between them or within them will generate sufficient tension. Setting is also crucial to the effect of a short story, but those written about the Vietnam War aren't always set in the jungle in the middle of a firefight. They may take place in basic training, at a Marine Corps hospital or back in hometown, U.S.A., but the war always directly influences the characters' motives and behavior.

Many short stories and novels are written in a standard, straightforward narrative. "The Interrogation of the Prisoner Bung by Sergeant Tree and Mister Hawkins", "Thi Bong Dzu," and "Wingfield," for example, start at the beginning of the events they focus on and progress chronologically through to the author's chosen end. Writing in a style that is familiar to their readers, Huddle, Rottmann, and Wolff depend primarily on careful character portrayal and subtle twist of plot to convey their messages.

Other stories, such as "The Ambush," "The Things They Carried," and "The First Clean Fact" use fragmented time shifts or an overload of poetic, in-country language as their dominant style. The key to these stories is to place the reader in a linguistic environment that resembles the war or the war's effects as closely as possible. Fiction in which time jumps back and forth, fantasy mixes with reality, and isolated incidents are depicted with unusual intensity is well qualified to represent the American soldiers' feelings of confusion and alienation.

Though there are those who say a fragmented story is too complex to persuade or affect the average reader, the literature of all wars offers both types of fiction. Sequential narratives are often easier to follow, easier for a reader to relate to. Yet surreal, dislocated narratives can absorb the reader with tone and images. Both styles, however, end up dealing with the same central issues of war: Fear, courage, death, technology, superstitions, boredom, camaraderie, movie heroes, and growing up— the loss of innocence.

And, as in most war literature, the most common central character in Vietnam War fiction is the basic grunt—the foot soldier. Because of his proximity to the fighting and his physical involvement in it, the infantryman epitomizes the soldier at war. There are stories written about pilots and cooks, nurses and generals, but not nearly as many pages have been devoted to them as to the average infantryman. He lives close to the land he fights in and depends more on himself and less on technology than any other fighter in modern warfare.

Finally, though, there is one major difference between the fiction of the Vietnam War and the fiction of other wars. The rites-of-passage concept, used in so many war stories, where the youth matures through experience into wise adulthood, seems inappropriate when dealing with Vietnam. Here the characters may mature, but too often also end up drug addicts, dead, or too alienated from society to function normally. At the very best, this war's veteran, like the narrator of "Wingfield," has accepted the experience and gone on with his life, visited only occasionally by shadows of the past. Perhaps it is through the stories of this war that light may be cast upon those shadows, illuminating them for the fictional character, the writer and the reader alike.

David Huddle
"The Interrogation of the Prisoner Bung by Mister Hawkins and Sergeant Tree"
1971

David Huddle, born in 1942, served in the U.S. Army from 1964 to 1967, first as a paratrooper in Germany, later as a Military Intelligence specialist in Vietnam. He has several books of poetry and short stories to his credit including A Dream With No Stump Roots In It, Paper Boy, *and* Only the Little Bone. *Huddle currently teaches literature and creative writing at the University of Vermont in Burlington, Vermont.*

The land in these provinces to the south of the capital city is so flat it would be possible to ride a bicycle from one end of this district to the other and to pedal only occasionally. The narrow highway passes over kilometers and kilometers of rice fields, laid out square and separated by slender green lines of grassy paddy-dikes and by irrigation ditches filled with bad water. The villages are far apart and small. Around them are clustered the little pockets of huts, the hamlets where the rice farmers live. The village that serves as the capital of this district is just large enough to have a proper marketplace. Close to the police compound, a detachment of Americans has set up its tents. These are lumps of new green canvas, and they sit on a concrete, French-built tennis court, long abandoned, not far from a large lily pond where women come in the morning to wash clothes and where policemen of the compound and their children come to swim and bathe in the late afternoon.

The door of a room to the rear of the District Police Headquarters is cracked for light and air. Outside noises—chickens quarreling, children playing, the mellow grunting of the pigs owned by the police chief— these reach the ears of the three men inside the quiet room. The room is not a cell; it is more like a small bedroom.

The American is nervous and fully awake, but he forces himself to yawn and sips at his coffee. In front of him are his papers, the report forms, yellow notepaper, two pencils and a ball-point pen. Across the table from the American is Sergeant Tree, a young man who was noticed by the government of his country and taken from his studies to be sent to interpreter's school. Sergeant Tree has a pleasant and healthy face.

He is accustomed to smiling, especially in the presence of Americans, who are, it happens, quite fond of him. Sergeant Tree knows that he has an admirable position working with Mister Hawkins; several of his unlucky classmates from interpreter's school serve nearer the shooting.

The prisoner, Bung, squats in the far corner of the room, his back at the intersection of the cool concrete walls. Bung is a large man for an Asian, but he is squatted down close to the floor. He was given a cigarette by the American when he was first brought into the room, but has finished smoking and holds the white filter inside his fist. Bung is not tied, nor restrained, but he squats perfectly still, his bare feet laid out flat and large on the floor. His hair, cut by his wife, is cropped short and uneven; his skin is dark, leathery, and there is a bruise below one of his shoulder blades. He looks only at the floor, and he wonders what he will do with the tip of the cigarette when the interrogation begins. He suspects that he ought to eat it now so that it will not be discovered later.

From the large barracks room on the other side of the building comes laughter and loud talking, the policemen changing shifts. Sergeant Tree smiles at these sounds. Some of the younger policemen are his friends. Hawkins, the American, does not seem to have heard. He is trying to think about sex, and he cannot concentrate.

"Ask the prisoner what his name is."

"What is your name?"

The prisoner reports that his name is Bung. The language startles Hawkins. He does not understand this language, except the first ten numbers of counting, and the words for yes and no. With Sergeant Tree helping him with the spelling, Hawkins enters the name into the proper blank.

"Ask the prisoner where he lives."

"Where do you live?"

The prisoner wails a string of language. He begins to weep as he speaks, and he goes on like this, swelling up the small room with the sound of his voice until he sees a warning twitch of the interpreter's hand. He stops immediately, as though corked. One of the police chief's pigs is snuffing over the ground just outside the door, rooting for scraps of food.

"What did he say?"

"He says that he is classed as a poor farmer, that he lives in the hamlet near where the soldiers found him, and that he has not seen his wife and his children for four days now and they do not know where he is.

"He says that he is not one of the enemy, although he has seen the enemy many times this year in his hamlet and in the village near his hamlet. He says that he was forced to give rice to the enemy on two different occasions, once at night, and another time during the day, and that he gave rice to the enemy only because they would have shot him if he had not.

"He says that he does not know the names of any of these men. He says that one of the men asked him to join them and to go with them, but that he told this man that he could not join them and go with them because he was poor and because his wife and his children would not be able to live without him to work for them to feed them. He says that the enemy men laughed at him when he said this but that they did not make him go with them when they left his house.

"He says that two days after the night the enemy came and took rice from him, the soldiers came to him in the field where he was working and made him walk with them for many kilometers, and made him climb into the back of a large truck, and put a cloth over his eyes, so that he did not see where the truck carried him and did not know where he was until he was put with some other people in a pen. He says that one of the soldiers hit him in the back with a weapon, because he was afraid at first to climb into the truck.

"He says that he does not have any money but that he has ten kilos of rice hidden beneath the floor of the kitchen of his house. He says that he would make us the gift of this rice if we would let him go back to his wife and his children."

When he has finished his translation of the prisoner's speech, Sergeant Tree smiles at Mister Hawkins. Hawkins feels that he ought to write something down. He moves the pencil to a corner of the paper and writes down his service number, his Social Security number, the telephone number of his girl friend in Silver Spring, Maryland, and the amount of money he has saved in his allotment account.

"Ask the prisoner in what year he was born."

Hawkins has decided to end the interrogation of this prisoner as quickly as he can. If there is enough time left, he will find an excuse for Sergeant Tree and himself to drive the jeep into the village.

"In what year were you born?"

The prisoner tells the year of his birth.

"Ask the prisoner in what place he was born."

"In what place were you born?"

The prisoner tells the place of his birth.

"Ask the prisoner the name of his wife."

"What is the name of your wife?"

Bung gives the name of his wife.

"Ask the prisoner the names of his parents."

Bung tells the names.

"Ask the prisoner the names of his children."

"What are the names of your children?"

The American takes down these things on the form, painstakingly, with the help in the spelling from the interpreter, who has become bored with this. Hawkins fills all the blank spaces on the front of the form. Later, he will add his summary of the interrogation in the space provided on the back.

"Ask the prisoner the name of his hamlet chief."

"What is the name of your hamlet chief?"

The prisoner tells this name, and Hawkins takes it down on the notepaper. Hawkins has been trained to ask these questions. If a prisoner gives one incorrect name, then all names given may be incorrect, all information secured unreliable.

Bung tells the name of his village chief, and the American takes it down. Hawkins tears off this sheet of notepaper and gives it to Sergeant Tree. He asks the interpreter to take this paper to the police chief to check if these are the correct names. Sergeant Tree does not like to deal with the police chief because the police chief treats him as if he were a farmer. But he leaves the room in the manner of someone engaged in important business. Bung continues to stare at the floor, afraid the American will kill him now that they are in this room together, alone.

Hawkins is again trying to think about sex. Again, he is finding it difficult to concentrate. He cannot choose between thinking about sex with his girl friend Suzanne or with a plump girl who works in a souvenir shop in the village. The soft grunting of the pig outside catches his ear, and he finds that he is thinking of having sex with the pig. He takes another sheet of notepaper and begins calculating the number of days he has left to remain in Asia. The number turns out to be one hundred and thirty-three. This distresses him because the last time he calculated the number it was one hundred and thirty-five. He decides to think about food. He thinks of an omelet. He would like to have an omelet. His eyelids begin to close as he considers all the things that he likes to eat: an omelet, chocolate pie, macaroni, cookies, cheeseburgers, black-cherry Jell-O. He has a sudden vivid image of Suzanne's stomach, the path of downy hair to her navel. He stretches the muscles in his legs, and settles into concentration.

The clamor of chickens distracts him. Sergeant Tree has caused this noise by throwing a rock on his way back. The police chief refused to speak with him and required him to conduct his business with the secretary, whereas this secretary gloated over the indignity to Sergeant Tree, made many unnecessary delays and complications before letting the interpreter have a copy of the list of hamlet chiefs and village chiefs in the district.

Sergeant Tree enters the room, goes directly to the prisoner, with the toe of his boot kicks the prisoner on the shinbone. The boot hitting bone makes a wooden sound. Hawkins jerks up in his chair, but before he quite understands the situation, Sergeant Tree has shut the door to the small room and has kicked the prisoner's other shinbone. Bung responds with a grunt and holds his shins with his hands, drawing himself tighter into the corner.

"Wait!" The American stands up to restrain Sergeant Tree, but this is not necessary. Sergeant Tree has passed by the prisoner now and has gone to stand at his own side of the table. From underneath his uniform shirt he takes a rubber club, which he has borrowed from one of his policeman friends. He slaps the club on the table.

"He lies!" Sergeant Tree says this with as much evil as he can force into his voice.

"Hold on now. Let's check this out." Hawkins' sense of justice has been touched. He regards the prisoner as a clumsy, hulking sort, obviously not bright, but clearly honest.

"The police chief says that he lies!" Sergeant Tree announces. He shows Hawkins the paper listing the names of the hamlet chiefs and the village chiefs. With the door shut, the light in the small room is very dim, and it is difficult to locate the names on the list. Hawkins is disturbed by the darkness, is uncomfortable being so intimately together with two men. The breath of the interpreter has something sweetish to it. It occurs to Hawkins that now, since the prisoner has lied to them, there will probably not be enough time after the interrogation to take the jeep and drive into the village. This vexes him. He decides there must be something unhealthy in the diet of these people, something that causes this sweet-smelling breath.

Hawkins finds it almost impossible to read the columns of handwriting. He is confused. Sergeant Tree must show him the places on the list where the names of the prisoner's hamlet chief and village chief are written. They agree that the prisoner has given them incorrect names, though Hawkins is not certain of it. He wishes these things were less complicated, and he dreads what he knows must follow. He thinks regretfully of what could have happened if the prisoner had given the correct names: the interrogation would have ended quickly, the prisoner released; he and Sergeant Tree could have driven into the village in the jeep, wearing their sunglasses, with the cool wind whipping past them, dust billowing around the jeep, shoeshine boys shrieking, the girl in the souvenir shop going with him into the back room for a time.

Sergeant Tree goes to the prisoner, kneels on the floor beside him, and takes Bung's face between his hands. Tenderly, he draws the prisoner's head close to his own, and asks, almost absentmindedly, "Are you one of the enemy?"

"No."

All this strikes Hawkins as vaguely comic, someone saying, "I love you," in a high-school play.

Sergeant Tree spits in the face of the prisoner and then jams the prisoner's head back against the wall. Sergeant Tree stands up quickly, jerks the police club from the table, and starts beating the prisoner with random blows. Bung stays squatted down and covers his head with both arms. He makes a shrill noise.

Hawkins has seen this before in other interrogations. He listens closely, trying to hear everything: little shrieks coming from Sergeant Tree's throat, the chunking sound of the rubber club makes. The American recognizes a kind of rightness in this, like the final slapping together of the bellies of a man and a woman.

Sergeant Tree stops. He stands, legs apart, facing the prisoner, his back to Hawkins. Bung keeps his squatting position, his arms crossed over his head.

The door scratches and opens just wide enough to let in a policeman friend of Sergeant Tree's, a skinny, rotten-toothed man, and a small boy. Hawkins has seen this boy and the policeman before. The two of them smile at the American and at Sergeant Tree, whom they admire for his education and for having achieved such an excellent position. Hawkins starts to send them back out, but decides to let them stay. He does not like to be discourteous to Asians.

Sergeant Tree acknowledges the presence of his friend and the boy. He sets the club on the table and removes his uniform shirt and the white T-shirt beneath it. His chest is powerful, but hairless. He catches Bung by the ears and jerks upward until the prisoner stands. Sergeant Tree is much shorter than the prisoner, and this he finds an advantage.

Hawkins notices that the muscles in Sergeant Tree's buttocks are clenched tight, and he admires this, finds it attractive. He has in his mind Suzanne. They are sitting on the back seat of the Oldsmobile. She has removed her stockings and garter belt, and now slides the panties down from her hips, down her legs, off one foot, keeping them dangling on one ankle, ready to be pulled up quickly in case someone comes to the car and catches them. Hawkins has perfect concentration. He sees her panties glow.

Sergeant Tree tears away the prisoner's shirt, first from one side of his chest and then the other. Bung's mouth sags open now, as though he were about to drool.

The boy clutches at the sleeve of the policeman to whisper in his ear. The policeman giggles. They hush when the American glances at them. Hawkins is furious because they have distracted him. He decides there is no privacy to be had in the entire country.

"Sergeant Tree, send these people out of here, please."

Sergeant Tree gives no sign that he has heard what Hawkins has said. He is poising himself to begin. Letting out a heaving grunt, Sergeant Tree chops with the police club, catching the prisoner directly in the center of the forehead. A flame begins in Bung's brain; he is conscious of a fire, blazing, blinding him. He feels the club touch him twice more, once at his ribs and once at his forearm.

"Are you the enemy?" Sergeant Tree screams.

The policeman and the boy squat beside each other near the door. They whisper to each other as they watch Sergeant Tree settle into the steady, methodical beating. Occasionally he pauses to ask the question again, but he gets no answer.

From a certain height, Hawkins can see that what is happening is profoundly sensible. He sees how deeply he loves these men in this room and how he respects them for the things they are doing. The knowledge rises in him, pushes to reveal itself. He stands up from his chair, virtually at attention.

A loud, hard smack swings the door wide open, and the room is filled with light. The Police Chief stands in the doorway, dressed in a crisp, white shirt, his rimless glasses sparkling. He is a fat man in the way that a good merchant might be fat—solid, confident, commanding. He stands with his hands on his hips, an authority in all matters. The policeman and the boy nod respectfully. The Police Chief walks to the table and picks up the list of hamlet chiefs and village chiefs. He examines this, and then he takes from his shirt pocket another paper, which is also a list of hamlet chiefs and village chiefs. He carries both lists to Sergeant Tree, who is kneeling in front of the prisoner. He shows Sergeant Tree the mistake he has made in getting a list that is out of date. He places the new list in Sergeant Tree's free hand, and then he takes the rubber club from Sergeant Tree's other hand and slaps it down across the top of Sergeant Tree's head. The Police Chief leaves the room, passing before the American, the policeman, the boy, not speaking or looking other than to the direction of the door.

It is late afternoon and the rain has come. Hawkins stands inside his tent, looking through the open flap. He likes to look out across the old tennis court at the big lily pond. He has been fond of water since he learned to water-ski. If the rain stops before dark, he will go out to join the policeman and the children who swim and bathe in the lily pond.

Walking out on the highway, with one kilometer still to go before he comes to the village, is Sergeant Tree. He is alone, the highway behind him and in front of him as far as he can see and nothing else around him but rain and the fields of wet, green rice. His head hurts and his arms are weary from the load of rice he carries. When he returned the prisoner to his hamlet, the man's wife made such a fuss Sergeant Tree had to shout at her to make her shut up, and then, while he was inside the prisoner's hut conducting the final arrangements for the prisoner's release, the rain came, and his policeman friends in the jeep left him to manage alone.

The ten kilos of rice he carries are heavy for him, and he would put his load down and leave it, except that he plans to sell the rice and add the money to what he has been saving to buy a .45 caliber pistol like the one Mister Hawkins carries at his hip. Sergeant Tree tries to think about how well-received he will be in California because he speaks the American language so well, and how it is likely that he will marry a rich American girl with very large breasts.

The prisoner Bung is delighted by the rain. It brought his children inside the hut, and the sounds of their fighting with each other make him happy. His wife came to him and touched him. The rice is cooking, and in a half hour his cousin will come, bringing with him the leader and two other members of Bung's squad. They will not be happy that half of their rice was taken by the interpreter to pay the American, but it will not be a disaster for them. The squad leader will be proud of Bung for gathering the information that he has—for he has memorized the guard routines at the police headquarters and at the old French area where the Americans are staying. He has watched all the comings and goings at these places, and he has marked out in his mind the best avenues of approach, the best escape routes, and the best places to set up ambush. Also, he has discovered a way that they can lie in wait and kill the Police Chief. It will occur at the place where the Police Chief goes to urinate every morning at a certain time. Bung has much information inside his head, and he believes he will be praised by the members of his squad. It is even possible that he will receive a commendation from someone very high.

His wife brings the rifle that was hidden, and Bung sets to cleaning it, savoring the smell of the rice his wife places before him and of the American oil he uses on the weapon. He particularly enjoys taking the weapon apart and putting it together again. He is very fast at this.

Asa Baber
"The Ambush"
1972

Born in Chicago, 1936, Asa Baber joined the Marine Corps in 1958, after graduating from Princeton University. In 1961, as an officer, he was briefly sent to Indochina while the United States considered invading Laos. After his military service, Baber received an M.A. from Northwestern University and an M.F.A. from the University of Iowa's Writers' Workshop. He has published one novel, The Land of a Million Elephants; *one play,* Goslings; *one short story collection,* Tranquility Base and other Stories by Asa Baber; *and numerous other articles, short stories, book reviews and columns. At the present time Baber is a contributing editor for* Playboy *magazine and teaches creative writing at Northwestern University.*

Here at Camp Pendleton it is summer even in winter and I dream of the grasshoppers. Here in sunny money land I listen to the singing and I wait to break, to crack like a cup and spill my soul. If I was not plunking my white-haired librarian it would be unbearable. She saves me as she straddles me. Do not be too superior, brothers, for you have not seen it all yet. Sometimes I think I have seen it all. Everything opens up and makes terrible sense and I want to die then.

Now out of Laos it has become a clean world again. The smells are gone. Even my rotting feet stay away from my nose. The malaria has retreated to my gall bladder, there to sleep. My brain is slowing down. They give me pills for that. I understand all the words spoken around me. There is no excuse for my sorrow except that I have heard the world crying and I have seen the strange alliances of nations and I think we are all filled with bile. When the doctors talk to me I say all this but they do not understand it.

There are cypress trees outside my window and across the road there is an artificial lake. The Engineers use that lake to build water obstacles and bridges. At dawn the sun lifts over the avocado orchards and gilts Vandergrift Boulevard. Then I can see the artillery trucks headed out towards Roblar Road and the firing ranges. All day the choppers and OE's fly over the hospital. They are noisy but they cannot stop the singing.

My room is in one of the white frame huts built at the beginning of World War I. It has venetian blinds that make prison shadows and a white rail bed and a print of a Utrillo on the wall. I do not know how a print like that found its way into a Marine Corps hospital. I hope it came with the room because I am sure many men have died in his room and it would be better to die looking at that street scene with the red splotch of paint on all that white. I do not plan to die here except on the bad days when the fever comes back and the dysentery hits again. When I cannot eat anything and my bowels pass water and blood I look at the Utrillo and think about dying.

They are very kind when they question me. I tell them it is screwed up over there. They will only listen to what they want to hear, both the Navy doctors and our own G-2. I try to tell them about the tangled things, that the French are strong with patrol leaders down to platoon level, that Russian civilian pilots are flying the airlift Ilyushins, that the North Vietnamese run the Fire Direction Centers. They listen to me and say yes yes we know all that. They know because they read reports. But it makes it a crazy war when you are over there.

Even Major Kline came by to see me. He lied to General Grider the night we were called out. Sutton and Devereux and I were lined up taking shots. They were pumping exotic vaccines into both my arms. Major Kline told the General we had been on a twelve hour alert. Yes sir they are ready yes sir the last shots of a series yes sir. Devereux got mad and said the last of a series like a one game World Series. The General knew somebody was lying but there was nothing they could do. We flew to Okinawa without calling anyone or saying goodby. I do not like Major Kline and he does not like me, but he owes me something and he knows it.

The grasshoppers come when I sleep. They have heads of dolphins and they buzz like locusts. They come from left to right across my dreams and always they chant we're coming to get you we're coming to get you. Then I try to wake up but I am too heavy for myself and I have to keep on dreaming while the grasshoppers hurt me. Sometimes I wake up screaming when I see Sutton with his non-head or Devereux with his wet intestines or Boun Kong in his burning skin.

I met my librarian when I was screaming one morning. It is better to sleep during the day because it is easier to wake up. She had brought books in a cart. She thought I was still asleep and she bent over me saying there there it's all right. I kept screaming so that she would not go away. She bent very close and I put my hands on her breasts. They felt like warm doves. She was not sure about me and she backed away. She was angry when she knew I was awake and she would not give me any books to read. Now she gives me all the books I want. She smells of quince and sharp things. She has blue eyes. She is only ten years older than I am but she has white hair.

What I want most is to have MatchKo scrubbing me. She knew all my tight nerves and muscles. Sutton loved her like he loved all the Okinawa whores. He was very immature about sex. He was always buying little personal presents for MatchKo. That last night at the baths he brought her a pearl and silver holly-leaf pin. He tried to bring it in to her while she was bathing me. She was pulling on me with the vibrator and oil and I was up in all my six by six glory. Sutton could not believe she would cheat on him. Not his MatchKo. His MatchKo of the rabbit warren and rice fields, his gold-toothed contortionist who had paid for her hut with God knows how many copulations. He stood there frozen and fearful while she manipulated me and winked at him. He threw the pin at her and ran out. He went north of Kadena to the native whorehouse area where no American should go. He was caught and tied by his feet to the back bumper of a taxi and dragged for miles with his head bouncing on the road. They dumped his body on a street in Naha. There was nothing left of his head but pulp. I saw it the next morning after Devereux and I spent the night looking for him.

Sutton was good in his job but stupid in life. He was one of the oldest Captains in the Marine Corps. They could not afford to get rid of him. He had all the languages they needed. He had French and Mandarin and Japanese. He knew some of the Meo dialect. If he had lived it might have helped us.

One of the doctors asked me if Sutton was queer. I said he was not more queer than some of the others. He wanted us to go to the baths and be rubbed down by MatchKo. He had lost a wife because he could make love only with whores. But that did not make him so different. There is a myth that the military is a masculine profession. I do not buy that. It is a profession where men dress for other men. Spit polish and web gear and linseed oil and starch and bleach. For my white-haired librarian I will clean and comb myself. For a commanding officer I will not go to much trouble. Sutton was sloppy in inspections but he dressed well when he went whoring. I do not think he was queer.

When Sutton was killed I was made c.o. of the Interrogation Team. We were attached to Task Force 116. We thought we were going into southern Laos. The panhandle area near Mahaxay and Tchepone covered Route Nationale 9. We had black and white lists and air recon maps. We were sent to Vientiane instead.

My room is as white as noise. The sheets and the bandages are white. I would like to see a calendar. It is either the end of February or the beginning of March. February is a cheating month so I hope it has finished. I do not think I will die this year because it is an odd year, 1961. I will die in an even year like my father and my grandfather.

The red-headed doctor asked me if I wanted to go back to Laos when I got better. He was not serious. I wanted to tell him how soft and fine a country it is with its rain forests dark and green all year.

The tree trunks are branchless. They are topped with lianas that hold ferns and orchids and wild figs. Walking through these forests you cannot see the sun. Flying over, you cannot see the forest floor. There are groves of small softwoods mixed with wild ginger, rhododendron and bamboo. There are coconut and areca palms and bananas. These forests shelter tigers, panthers, elephants, deer. When there is a war, our newspapers call these forests "jungles."

I cannot tell the doctor what it is like there because his spirit is not me. If I could go back without bearing arms or a colonial message, I would.

I often see the *phi* of Sutton and Devereaux and Boun Kong. They are wandering the earth and they will always be with me. They are also back in Laos in the Meo country. They are harvesting the poppies now. They are lucky; a *phi* can be two places at once. The plants are waist high now, in full bloom of rose or white or blue or mauve. I would like to be back at the harvest before the pale-green stems of the poppies are cut. The women go to the fields before the dew lifts. They collect the sap and dry it and wrap it in banana leaves. The brown blocks of raw opium are sold for very little in Zieng Khouang Province, and for a lot in Saigon.

The *phi* are strong spirits. They must always be honored. They are in the trees and mountains and rivers. They are in every human being and every dead person. I think it was Sutton's *phi* that came as a goat to warn us.

Go north of Vientiane on the royal Road, Route Coloniale 13. For twenty miles there are flat paddies and thickets and the sky is open. Then you climb to Ban Namone as the road circles and becomes covered with forest. Here are the lowland people. They are not good fighters. Pull them into combat and they will shoot their rifles into the air. To teach them to shoot to kill, you must set up targets, let them fire one shot at the target, walk them to the target and show them the bullet hole, go back and shoot one shot again. Their houses are on stilts. Pigs and chickens live under them. The men sleep most of the day and the women grow only enough rice to survive. These lowland dwellers will be the last people to fight for anything. They are the first people the Americans tried to indoctrinate.

After Ban Namone comes the valley of Vang Vieng. Here the road starts to climb steeply, through Ban Pha Tang, Ban Thieng, Muong Kassy. At Sala Phou Khoun, the road to the Plain of Jars goes east, Route Nationale 7.

All of these roads were built under the supervision of the French. The French also collected taxes and rice and salt and women under their "protectorate" which lasted for many generations. The French set the image for the white man. A white man is a Frenchman, a colonialist. A white man is diseased, as anything white in Asia must be diseased, whether it is spoiled buffalo meat or moldy fruit or human flesh.

In the mountains near the Plain of Jars live the fighters, the Meo. They build their houses on the ground. They are great hunters and riflemen and horsemen. They live off the land. They eat corn, cabbage, eggplant, onions, and the produce of their hunt. They live long lives doctored by the gall of bear and python, marrow of tiger, deer's soft horn. Devereux had worked with the Meo before Dien Bien Phu when he was attached to the French. He wanted to get back to them and he got permission for the two of us to go. We had to travel in civvies and an unmarked quarter-ton and we had to take a government driver. His name was Boun Kong. He drank *choum*, a rice wine, through a straw while he drove. He strapped a transister radio to the emergency brake and gave us a bumpy rock and roll concert.

After the turn at Sala Phou Khoun we were in no-man's land. We drank the wine. Devereux even stopped calling me lieutenant. I think it was the last happy time of my life.

When Boun Kong saw the goat he stopped the jeep. He was drunk and he tried to back the jeep while staring at the goat. It was a very dignified goat and it walked slowly across the road without looking at us. Devereux yelled allons allons and Boun Kong backed the jeep even farther saying c'est impossible c'est impossible c'est La Morte. Devereux stood up in the back seat and slapped Boung Kong on the ears. I jumped out and ran at the goat. That is when they hit us. They probably thought I had seen them.

There was the great horrible compression of air and dust and noise. I don't think they used any launchers or grenades. They wanted the jeep. But they had .50's and their own Chinese weapons and they aimed high to spare the chassis. We hadn't come all the way into their setup. They had gotten behind us. They opened up a little too early. Everything hit Devereux's belly. He folded and fell out. I ran into the brush. I am ashamed I ran, but there was not anything I could do. Sometimes the doctors pushed me on this. They think I wanted to be a hero. Boun Kong tried to be a hero. He wanted to throw the extra jerry-can of gas at them. It bounced against his leg as he carried it a few steps down the road. The bullets were cracking and spitting around him. I rolled on down the slope and heard an explosion. Then there was that deep silence after battle when the eardrum vibrates and the balance slowly returns. I kept my head down. I heard one of them sweeping through the grass. He stopped near me but he did not shoot. I raised my head and he looked at me. He was a white man, perhaps French or Russian. He fired a few shots down the gulley and climbed back to his platoon of gooks. They wanted the jeep. They took it.

I crawled back to the road. Boun Kong was still burning. Devereux's guts were in his hands. He had died looking surprised. I went into the brush. I did not start to walk back until it was night. I did not use the road because I was afraid of it. It took me three days before I reached the road north of Vientiane.

Here in Camp Pendleton the blinds are raised each day and the sunlight comes into this bleached vanilla room. There are deer running through the sage in the canyons near San Clemente. You can walk the firebreaks on the ridgeline and hunt the deer. I will not ever be a good hunter again because my hands shake now. The doctors give me pills for it and say I will get over it. I do not think so. My hands shake because I have to fight the grasshoppers and listen to the singing. That makes me tired. The singing is always in the back of my head. I do not know what song they are singing. It is a march with a steady rhythm and stamping feet and many voices. It is not pleasant and sometimes they stop singing and they shout.

Larry Rottmann
"Thi Bong Dzu"
1973

Larry Rottmann, who was born in 1942, served in the U.S. Army as an infantryman from 1965-1968. His tour of duty in Vietnam was from 1967-1968. Other works by Rottmann include a novel, American Eagle: The Story of Navajo Vietnam Veteran, *and* A History of the 25th Infantry Division in Vietnam. *He has published dozens of poems in newspapers and magazines and contributed to many poetry and short story collections. Rottmann is also co-author of several plays and a contributing editor to* Winning Hearts and Minds: War Poems by Vietnam Veterans *and* Free Fire Zone: Short Stories by Vietnam Veterans. *Currently Rottmann teaches English at Southwest Missouri State University in Springfield, Missouri.*

It was the day before his birthday, and Thi Bong Dzu was a little bit excited. However, he knew it was important that he keep such feelings to himself, for if he failed to control his emotions, he could compromise the entire unit's mission that night.

Dzu rose early, for he had a lot of other work to do before the pre-arranged meeting time. Since the death of his father nearly six months before, Dzu had been the man-of-the-house to his mother, three younger sisters, and grandmother. As he crossed the packed earth of the yard on his way to the well, he could see faint luminescent trails of parachute flares low in the northeast sky. And a moment later, from somewhere in the south near Saigon, came the groundshuddering rumble of a B-52 bomb raid.

Drawing a full bucket, and holding his breath, Dzu doused himself with the cool water. He soaped his lean body vigorously, rinsed off with a couple more buckets, and shaking dry, trotted back to the hut shivering a little in the chill morning air.

He dressed quickly, pulling on a pair of faded trousers, a much-mended shirt, and his sandals, which he'd made himself from some rope and an old jeep tire. Moving quietly, so as not to wake his family, Dzu started a small fire in the cooking pit just outside the door. Into a battered tin pot he placed a few handfuls of rice, a few tiny dried minnows, and a bit of salt. He placed the pot on the low fire, and stirred it slowly until little bubbles started to appear. Dumping a small amount into a chipped bowl, he began eating it, pinching the rice between his thumb and forefinger.

As he ate, he watched the huge, blood-red ball of sun rise slowly. The air remained cool, and a thick mist hovered low over the flooded paddies surrounding the house. The sky was clear though, and Dzu knew that within the hour it would be steaming hot. Worse yet, the sky would probably still be clear that night. He frowned slightly at this prospect, for it would make their operation all the more difficult.

Swallowing the last few bites of breakfast, Dzu gently began to wake his family (all except grandmother, who'd been known to bite anyone who interrupted her sleep). As his mother and sisters began to move about, he took the rice sickle from the tool shelf, and squatting on the stoop, began to sharpen its well-worn cutting edge with a small sandstone. Back and forth, back and forth he moved the stone along the gentle curve of the blade, recalling how he had always been fascinated by the way his father had done it. Back and forth, back and forth, Dzu felt himself slipping into an almost hypnotic rhythm. Suddenly he was snapped from his near trance by a loud squawk from grandmother, who'd been playfully awakened by Dzu's sisters. Testing the sickle's edge, he was surprised to see a fine red line appear on his thumb where he'd drawn it across the steel. Satisfied, he replaced the sharpening stone and made ready to leave for the fields.

His mother had put some of the cooked rice in a small bucket, along with a piece of bread, for lunch. As Dzu took it from her, she noticed the blood on his thumb, and made him sit down while she washed out the cut and tied a too-large bandage around it. Dzu realized that she was making a lot of fuss over nothing, but he knew she was trying to let him know how much she loved him. Because he was now the head of the family, it wouldn't do for her to kiss him or fawn over him, so she expressed her concern in subtle, less obvious ways, like all this bother over a small cut.

But it was getting late, and already Dzu could see the other men of the hamlet heading for the fields. During rice harvest, no time could be wasted, for he was anxious to get started, especially since he'd have to stop a little early that day in order to get ready for the mission. He kissed each of his sisters, made a face at grandmother who was still grouching around, and took off down the path.

Dzu felt good, and for the second time allowed himself to think about his upcoming birthday. He knew that no matter how early he arose the next day, his mother would already be up, fixing a special breakfast. Even though they didn't have much, she would always manage to come up with a small bit of eel, some extra spices, or even fresh melons on birthdays. The girls would have some small, but hand-made and priceless, gift—like the red scarf from his last birthday that he wore on patrols. And even grandmother, despite her pretended gruffness, would have something for him too. But Dzu cared less for the presents than the special feeling of closeness that came on birthdays. Their home always seems to have extra warmth and happiness then.

Dzu's thoughts were suddenly jarred by the roar of tanks. The path to the paddies paralleled Route 13, and a long U.S. convoy was approaching. Dzu paused as the vehicles rumbled by, and remembered the first armored task force that had passed his village, and how, as a small boy, he had stood clutching his father, frozen by fear at the sight of the seemingly endless parade of huge war machines. He recalled how the calloused hands of his father had trembled with fright, and yet how his jaw had clinched in anger and hatred. And he would never forget the words his usually quiet father had spat out at the disappearing Americans: "Bastards! Murderers! Animals!"

At that time, Dzu didn't know what it was that had caused his father to react so vehemently to the hairy strangers, but now he knew. As he watched the column roll by, and carefully counted the number of tanks, APC's, and supply trucks, he remembered the first air strike on his hamlet. The black, screaming planes had suddenly knifed through an overcast sky one afternoon, and for almost an hour had raked Ben Cat with rockets, cannon fire, bombs, and napalm. In the attack, Dzu lost his older brother, his grandfather, two cousins, and a half-dozen playmates. The village's market place, temple, school—as well as over half its homes—were destroyed. Almost half the villagers were killed or wounded, and many still carried the scars caused by the sticking fire. That night most of the hamlet's able-bodied men joined the 271st Viet Cong Regiment. Dzu's father was among the volunteers, and he participated in many operations against the enemy. He was a brave fighter, and at the time of his death during the attack of an artillery fire support base, was still recovering from a wound suffered in an earlier action.

When his father was killed, Dzu took his place not only as head of the household, but also as a scout for the 271st recon platoon. In less than six months he had participated in nineteen separate engagements, had been decorated for bravery twice, and had risen from private to corporal. The platoon had lost nearly a third of its original men during that period, but had also recorded several surprising victories, each time against overwhelming odds and firepower. Dzu was the only man in the unit who hadn't been wounded, and had come to be regarded by them as something of a good luck charm. "Keep bullet holes out of Thi's shirt and we'll all be safe" was a frequently heard remark within the platoon.

Dzu's pulse was pounding as the end of the column approached. He thought of the night's mission and a bitter smile formed on his lips. As the last tank, laden with GI's, passed, Dzu raised his hand in a mock salute. One of the soldiers on the vehicle shouted "Hey, gook, you want smoke-smoke?" and laughing, threw a pack of C-Ration cigarettes at him. Grabbing them out of the air, Dzu stripped off the cellophane, removed the cigarettes, and turned the pack inside out. Taking a pencil stub from his pocket, he scribbled down the unit designations and makeup of the convoy. He folded the small paper, tucked it away, and puffing on one of the stale Camels, strode off down the path, his lunch pot and sickle flapping against his thin legs.

Arriving at the fields a few minutes later, Dzu stripped down to his shorts and went right to work. Again and again the sickle flashed in its smooth arc, severing the heavily laden stalks of rice from their submerged roots. With each easy swing, another sheave would slide neatly into Dzu's crooked left arm. When the shock felt exactly the right size and weight, he tied it about the middle with a piece of twine and laid it on the dike, away from the water. He worked tirelessly, his spare frame bent almost double and his legs immersed in water to mid-calf. He loved the squishy feel of the mud around his toes, and the rough tickle of the stubby, already cut-off rice shoots.

Dzu worked without a break until a little past mid-day. When he finally paused, he looked at the pile of shocks and realized he had already finished the day's quota. Taking his lunch, he walked to the bank of the nearby Hoc Mon River and sat down to eat. On the opposite bank, a young man about his age was fishing with a long, limber bamboo pole. It looked like the fish were biting well, but they were apparently too quick for the fisherman. Each time the float bobbed, he'd jerk the pole, but all he ever came up with was an empty hook which he'd rebait and throw back in. "Xin loi" laughed Dzu, "Too bad." For a moment he felt sorry for himself, wishing that he too could try his luck at catching the elusive cam roa. Perhaps on his birthday...? But that thought lasted only a moment. Dzu remembered his responsibility to his family and to the liberation, and chided himself for such selfish reverie.

He finished his bread and rice and stretched out under a low pineapple scrub for a two-hour nap, just as he had done every day of his life. He knew the strength of the afternoon sun, and wondered to himself why only monkeys and U.S. soldiers dared defy it. He noted many similarities between the two, and was in the process of enumerating them when he fell asleep.

Dzu woke with a start to find his uncle standing over him, pointing a stick at his head and shouting, "Bang, bang, you're dead, you dirty Vee Cee!" "Don't make bad jokes, Uncle." Dzu replied as he jumped to his feet. Angry because he had allowed himself to be sneaked up on, Dzu grabbed the stick "gun," threw it into the stream, and without a backward glance, ran over to the road where his uncle's ox-car was sitting and led the big water buffalo off toward the paddy.

When Dzu arrived at his pile of shocks, he immediately began tossing them one by one into the cart. By the time uncle had walked over from the river, they were all loaded but one. Dzu paused for a long moment, scanning the horizon and listening intently for the "whack-whack" of patrolling helicopters. Taking the remaining shock, he walked out to the middle of the paddy. He felt around a moment with his feet, then with a swift motion snatched an oblong object wrapped in plastic from beneath the water and concealed it within the rice bundle. Dzu placed this shock deep in the middle of the loaded cart, slipped into his shirt, and calling to his uncle, "Make sure you deliver that load on time," he headed down the path for home.

As he made his way back to the village, Dzu noted that it was beginning to cloud up a little to the east. "A good sign," he thought to himself, and quickened his pace. His sisters saw him coming from a long way off, and ran to meet him. He was pleased, for he loved them dearly, but he also knew that part of their jubilance was due to their sharing of his birthday "secret." He embraced them all as they descended upon him in a maelstrom of laughter, and with one girl holding each hand and one riding piggy-back, he trotted the last hundred meters or so to the house. Shouting and giggling, they burst into the yard, almost tumbling over grandmother. "Not a very grownup way for the head of the house to behave," she groused, but she knew of Dzu's mission that night, and so she said no more.

A few minutes later mother returned from the market place where she'd been shopping for a breakfast treat. Out of sight of the girls, she handed Dzu a tai tom. He opened the hollow pineapple, removed the two dozen .45 caliber shells that had been hidden inside, and with an oily rag, carefully cleaned each one. Moving the sleeping platform to one side, he uncovered the entrance to a small tunnel. Wrapping the bullets in the rag, he put them in the families' tiny bomb shelter, then replaced the bed and went outside for supper.

Everyone else was in a gay mood during the meal, but Dzu couldn't keep his mind on the swirling conversation. He kept running over the plans for the night and casting anxious glances at the clearing sky. As they finished their supper, uncle arrived with the load of rice. Dzu removed his special bundle and took it inside while the rest of the family helped unload the cart. He again moved the bed and dropped into the tunnel beneath it. By the light of a small candle he unwrapped his package. With the skill that comes only from long practice, he broke the submachinegun down into its various parts and cleaned and recleaned each one. When he was satisfied that the weapon was spotless, he lightly oiled each piece, then quickly reassembled it. He also loaded his two magazines with the recently acquired cartridges.

Emerging from the tunnel, he could see that it was nearly dark outside, and time for him to leave. Dzu put on his black cotton shirt and pants, and a pair of black rubber-soled shoes. He tied the red scarf around his neck and fastened two hand grenades to his belt. He locked one loaded magazine into the gun and stuck the other in his waistband for easy access. Choosing a moment when the girls were busy at play, he slipped outside, and after pausing only long enough to make sure mother had replaced the bed, Dzu disappeared into the darkness.

Alert and careful, Dzu padded silently along the path toward the rendezvous point. The sky was again overcast, and a thick fog was forming along the ground. Dzu's spirits rose, and he anticipated another successful operation. He felt sure he would be home in plenty of time to get some sleep before his birthday breakfast. Dzu started thinking about grumpy grandmother and didn't see the first soldier's slight movement. He was imagining the antics of his sisters and didn't hear the faint click of the safety on the second GI's rifle. He was seeing the shy smile of his proud mother and didn't feel the tug of the flare trip-wire until too late.

Dzu stood paralyzed by the sudden explosive blaze of light, and in the instant before his body was riddled by the bullets of two machine guns and a dozen M-16s; in that half-moment before thousands of razor-sharp fragments from Claymores and grenades tore at his flesh, Dzu realized that he wasn't ever going to have another birthday. He realized that he was never going to be twelve.

Shirley Ann Grau
"The Homecoming"
1973

After attending Tulane University Shirley Ann Grau primarily has devoted her career to writing. Her works include The Black Prince and Other Stories; The Wind Shifting West; The Keepers of the House, *which won a Pulitzer Prize in 1968;* The Condor Passes; *and her most recent collection,* Nine Women.

The telegram was in the middle of the dining room table. It was leaning against the cut-glass bowl that sometimes held oranges, only this week nobody had bought any. There was just the empty bowl, lightly dust coated and flecked with orange oil. And the telegram.
"Did you have to put it there?" Susan asked her mother.
"It's nothing to be ashamed of," her mother said.
"I'm not ashamed," she said, "But why did you put it there?"
"It's something to be proud of."
"It looks just like a sign."
"People will want to see it," her mother said.
"Yes," Susan said, "I guess they will."

She took her time dressing, deliberately. Twice her mother called up the stairs, "Susan, hurry. I told people any time after three o'clock."
And they were prompt, some of them anyway. (How many had her mother asked? She'd been such a long time on the phone this morning...) Susan heard them come, heard their voices echo in the high-ceilinged hall, heard the boards creak with unaccustomed weight. She could follow their movements in the sounds of the old boards. As clearly as if she were looking at them, she knew that the women had stayed inside and the men had moved to the porches.

Wide porches ran completely around two sides of the house, south and west. "Porches are best in old houses like this," her mother often said. "Good, useful porches."

The west porch was the morning porch. Its deep overhang kept off the sun even in these July afternoons. There was a little fringe of moonflower vine too, across the eaves, like lace on a doily. The big white moonflowers opened each night like white stars and each morning, like squashed bugs, dropped to the ground. They were trained so carefully on little concealed wires up there that they never once littered the porch...The south porch was the winter porch. The slanted winter sun always reached that side, bare and clear, no vines, no planting. A porch for old people. Where the winter sun could warm their thin blood, and send it pumping through knotty blue veins. Her grandmother sat out there, sightless in the sun, all one winter. Every good day, every afternoon until she died....

Susan always thought one porch was much bigger until she measured them—carefully, on hands and knees, with a tape measure. How funny, she thought; they seemed so different to be just the same.

On this particular afternoon, as Susan came downstairs—slowly, reluctantly, hesitating at each step—she glanced toward the sound of men's voices on the south porch. Looking through the screen into the light, she saw no faces, just the glaring dazzle of white shirts. She heard the little rattle of ice in their glasses and she smelled the faint musty sweet odor of bourbon.

Like a wake, she thought. Exactly like a wake.

Her mother called: "In the dining room, dear."

There was coffee on the table, and an ice bucket and a bottle of sherry and two bottles of bourbon. "Come in, Susan" her mother said. "The girls are here to see you."

Of course, Susan thought. They had to be first, her mother's best friends, Mrs. Benson and Mrs. Watkins, each holding a sherry glass. Each kissed her, each with a puff of faint flower scent from the folds of their flowered dresses. "We are so sorry, Susan," they said one after the other.

Susan started to say thank you and then decided to say nothing.

Mrs. Benson peered over her sherry glass at the telegram propped on the table next to the good silver coffeepot. "I thought the Defense Department sent them," she said, "that's what I have always heard."

Susan's mother said emphatically, her light voice straining over the words, just the way it always did: "They sent me one for my husband."

"That's right." Mrs. Watkins nodded. "I saw it just now when I came in. Right under the steps in the hall. In that little gold frame."

"When I read that telegram," Susan's mother said, "I got a pain in my heart that I never got rid of. I carried that pain in my heart from that day to this."

And Susan said, patiently explaining: "The army told Harold's parents."

"And the Carters sent word to you, her mother said firmly. Her hand with its broad wedding band flapped in the air. "There on the table, that's the word they sent."

All of a sudden Susan's black dress was too hot and too tight. She was perspiring all over it. She would ruin it, and it was her good dress.

"I'm so hot," she said. "I've got to change to something lighter."

Her mother followed her upstairs. "You're upset," she said, "but you've got to control yourself."

"The way you controlled yourself," Susan said.

"You're mocking now, but that's what I mean, I had to control myself, and I've learned.

"I've nothing to control," Susan said. She stripped off the black dress. The wet fabric stuck and she jerked it free. Close to her ear, a couple of threads gave a little screeching rip. "I've got to find something lighter. It's god-awfully hot down there."

"White," her mother said. "White would be correct."

Susan looked at her, shrugged, and took a white pique out of the closet.

"Are you all right?"

"I'm fine," Susan said, "I'm great."

She put the white pique dress across a chair and sat down on her bed. Its springs squeaked gently. She stretched out and stared up at the crocheted tester and felt her sweat-moistened skin turn cool in the air. She pulled her slip and her bra down to her waist and lay perfectly still.

Abruptly she thought: If there were a camera right over me, it would take a picture of five eyes: the two in my head, the one in my navel, and the two on my breasts. Five eyes staring up at the ceiling.

She rolled over on her stomach.

It was a foolish thing to think. Very foolish. She never seemed to have the proper thoughts or feelings. Her mother now, she had the right thoughts, everybody knew they were right. But Susan didn't . . .

Like now. She ought to be more upset now. She ought to be in tears over the telegram. She'd found it stuck in the crack of the door this morning. "Have been informed Harold was killed at Quang Tri last Thursday." She should have felt something. When her mother got the news of her father's death in Korea, the neighbors said you could hear her scream for a block; they found her huddled on the floor, stretched out flat and small as she could be with the bulging womb that held an almost completed baby named Susan.

Susan lifted her head and looked at the picture on her night table. It was a colored photograph of her father, the same one her mother had painted into a portrait to hang over the living room fireplace. Susan used to spend hours staring into that small frame, trying to sharpen the fuzzy colored lines into the shape of a man. She'd never been quite able to do that; the only definite thing she knew about him was the sharp white lines of his grave marker in Arlington.

"That picture looks just exactly like him," her mother would say. "I almost think he'll speak to me. I'm so glad you can know what your father looked like."

And Susan never said: I still don't know. I never will.

And this whole thing now, her mourning for Harold, it was wrong. All wrong. She hadn't even known him very well. He was just a nice boy from school, a tall thin boy who worked in the A&P on Saturdays and liked to play pool on Sundays, who had a clear light tenor and sang solo parts with her in the glee club. His father worked for the telephone company and they lived on the other side of town on Millwood Street—she knew that much. He'd finished high school a year ago and he'd asked her to his senior prom, though she hadn't expected him to. On the way home, he offered her his class ring. "You can take it," he said. She could see his long narrow head in the light from the porch. "Till I get out of the army."

"Or some other girl wants it."

"Yeah."

Because she couldn't think of anything else, she said: "Okay, I'll keep it for you. If you want it, just write and I'll send it to you."

That was how she got the ring. She never wore it, and he didn't ask for it back. She didn't even see him again. His family moved away to the north part of the state, to Laurel, and Harold went there on his leaves. He didn't come back to town and he didn't call her. He did send a chain to wear the ring on—it was far too big for her finger—from California. She wrote him a thank-you note the very same day. But he didn't answer, and the ring and the chain hung on the back of her dresser mirror. He was just a boy whose ring she was keeping.

Maybe he'd told his parents something more. Why else would they wire her? And what had he told them? All of a sudden there were things she couldn't ask. The world had changed while she wasn't looking.

And Harold Carter was killed. Harold was the name of an English king, and he was killed somewhere too. Now there was another Harold dead. How many had there been in between? Thousands of Harolds, thousands of different battles...

Her mother opened the door so quickly it slipped from her hand and smashed into the wall. The dresser mirror shivered and the class ring swung gently on its chain. "Susan, I thought, I just thought of something..."

What, Susan asked silently. Did you forget the extra ice? Something like that? Will people have to have warm drinks?

"You're acting very strangely. I've never seen you act like this...Did something go on that shouldn't have? Tell me."

Susan tossed a hairbrush from hand to hand. "Maybe it's me," she said, "but I just don't know what people are talking about any more."

"All right," her mother said, "you make me put it this way. Are you going to have a baby?"

Susan stared at the broken edges of the bristles, and she began to giggle. "Harold left a year ago, Mother."

"Oh," her mother said, "oh, oh, oh." And she backed out the door.

Susan said after her, sending her words along the empty hall where there was nobody to hear them: "That was you who was pregnant. And it was another war."

She put on some more perfume; her flushed skin burned at its touch. She glanced again at the photograph of her father.

You look kind of frozen there. But then I guess you really are. Frozen at twenty-three. Smile and crooked cap and all.

And Susan remembered her grandmother sitting on the porch in the sun, eyes hooded like a bird's, fingers like birds' claws. Senility that came and went, like a shade going up and down. "He don't look nothing like the pictures, she said. She always called her dead son-in-law he, never used his name. "Never looked like that, not dead, not alive." The one hand that was not paralyzed waved at an invisible fly. "Died and went to glory, that boy. Those pictures your mother likes, they're pictures of him in glory. Nothing more nor less than glory."

The old woman was dead now too. There weren't any pictures of her. She'd gone on so long she fell apart, inch by inch of skin. All the dissolution visible outside the grave...

Susan breathed on the glass front of her father's picture and polished it with the hem of her slip. The young glorious dead...like Harold. Only she didn't have a picture of Harold. And she didn't really remember what he looked like.

She could hear the creak of cane rockers on the porch, the soft mumbling of men's talk. She stood by the screen to listen.

"I'll tell you." Harry Benson, the druggist, was sitting on the big chair, the one with the fancy scrolled back. "They called us an amphibious unit and put us ashore and they forgot about us. Two weeks with nothing to do but keep alive on that beach."

That would be Okinawa. She had heard about his Okinawa.

"And after a while some of the guys got nervous. If they found a Jap still alive they'd work him over good, shoot him seven or eight times, just to see him jump. They kind of thought it was fun, I guess."

"Hold it a minute, Harry," Ed Watkins, who was the railroad agent, said. "Here's Susan."

They both stood up. They'd never done that before.

"We were talking about our wars, honey," Mr. Benson said. "I'm afraid we were."

"That's all right," Susan said. "I don't mind."

"It was crazy, plain crazy," Mr. Watkins said. "Like that guy, must been '51 or '52."

"Ed, look," Mr. Benson said. "Maybe we ought to stop talking about this."

"Nothing so bad...This guy, I don't think I ever knew his name, he was just another guy. And in those days you remember how they came down in waves from the North. You could hear them miles away, yelling and blowing horns. So, this time, you could hear them like always, and this guy, the one I didn't know a name for, he puts a pistol right under his jaw and blows the top of his head off. The sergeant just looked at him, and all he can say is, 'Jesus Christ, that son of a bitch bled all over my gun.' "

"Hard to believe things like that now," Mr. Benson said.

"I believe them," Susan said. "Excuse me, I have something to do in the kitchen."

She had to pass through the dining room. Mrs. Benson still had a sherry glass in her hand, her cheeks were getting flushed and her eyes were very bright. Mrs. Watkins had switched from sherry to whiskey and was putting more ice in her highball. Susan's mother poured herself coffee.

Susan thought: Mrs. Benson's going to have an awful sherry hangover and Mrs. Watkins' ulcer is going to start hurting from the whiskey and my mother's drunk about twenty cups of coffee today and that's going to make her sick...

She only said, "I'm just passing through."

But she found herself stopping to look at the telegram. At the shape of the letters and the way they went on the page. At the way it was signed: "Mr. and Mrs. Carter." She thought again how strange that was. They were both big hearty people—"Call me Mike," Mr. Carter said to all the kids. "We're Mike and Ida here." Now all of a sudden they were formal.

Like a wedding invitation, Susan thought suddenly. Only just the opposite.

She reached out and touched the paper. It crackled slightly under her fingers. She went on rubbing her thumb across the almost smooth surface, watching the sweat of her skin begin to stain the yellow paper. A little stain, a little mark, but one that would grow if she kept at it.

That was the end of Harold Carter, she thought. He ended in the crisp, crunchy feel of a piece of paper. A tall thin boy who'd taken her to a dance and given her a ring that was too big for her. All that was left of him was a piece of paper.

She'd send the ring back to his parents. Maybe they'd like to have it.

Or maybe they'd rather she kept it. But keeping it would be keeping him. All of a sudden she saw the ring hanging on the side of her dresser mirror, and she looked into its blue stone and way down in its synthetic depths she saw a tiny little Harold, germ-sized and far away. As she looked he winked out.

She put the telegram down. "I really was just going to the kitchen."

"You're not wearing your ring." Mrs. Watkins said.

"No," she said, "no, I never did wear it."

"You must be so upset." Mrs. Benson sipped delicately at the edge of the yellow sherry. "Just like your poor mother."

"I wasn't married to him," Susan said, "it's different."

Her mother was standing next to her, hand on her shoulder. "You would have married him."

"No," Susan said, "no, I don't think so."

"Of course you would have. Her mother was firm. "Why else would he have given you the ring?"

Susan started to say: Because he didn't have anybody else to give it to and he couldn't give it to his mother.

Her mother went on patting her shoulder. "We should be proud of them, Susan. Harold was a fine young man."

Was he? She didn't have the heart to say that aloud either. Did he shoot people to see them squirm? Did he pull the trigger against his own head with fear?

"The young men are so heroic," her mother said. The two women murmured consent. Her mother would know; her mother had lost a husband in a war, she would know.

All the brave young men that die in their glory, Susan thought. And leave rings to girls they hardly knew, and pictures on mantels in houses where they never lived. Rings that don't fit and pictures that don't resemble them.

"Harold was an English king," she said aloud.

"Yes, dear," her mother said patiently. "That's history."

Harold Carter didn't get to sit on porches and remember, the way Watkins and Benson were doing now. He hadn't got to do anything, except go to high school and die. But then, you didn't really know that either, Susan thought. You really didn't know what he did out there, what memories he might have brought back inside his head.

Mrs. Watkins repeated, "All the young men are so brave."

"No," Susan said abruptly. "Not my father, and not Harold. They weren't brave, they just got caught."

In the silence she could hear the soft wheeze of their astonished breaths, and, as she turned, the creak of old boards under her heel. "They don't die in glory." The words came out sounding like her speech at the Senior Debating Society. "They just die dead. Anyway, I was on my way to fix a cup of tea."

Nobody followed her to the kitchen, just the little ribbon of sound from her high heels on the bare boards and linoleum. She flipped on the fire under the kettle, decided it would take too long and began to heat some water in a pan. Her feet hurt; she kicked off her shoes. The water warmed and she poured it over the instant tea. There were no lemons in the refrigerator; she remembered suddenly that there weren't any oranges on the dining room table either, that today had been marketing day and nobody had gone.

She put sugar in the tea and tasted it. It was barely warm and nasty, salty almost. She'd forgotten to rinse the dishes again. She would drink it anyway, while she made another proper cup. She put the flame back under the kettle. She pushed open the screen door and went out on the kitchen porch.

It was very small, just wide enough for one person to pass between the railing and the garbage can that always stood there. She'd often argued with her mother over that. "Put it in the yard, it just brings flies into the house." "A clean can," her mother said, "does not attract flies." And the can stayed.

She sat down on the railing, wondering if it would leave a stripe on her white dress. She decided she didn't care. She sipped the cold tea and stared out into the back yard, at the sweet peas growing along the wire fence, at the yellow painted boards on the house next door.

She was still staring over there, not seeing anything in particular, not thinking anything at all, when Mr. Benson came around the corner of the house. He walked across the back yard and stopped, finally, one foot on the bottom step.

"You left the girls in quite a state back there," he said.

So they had rushed to the porch to tell the men...Susan didn't take her eyes off the sweet peas, the soft gentle colors of the sweet peas. "They get upset real easy."

"I reckon they do," he said, "and they quiet down real easy too."

She began to swing her leg slowly. I shouldn't have left my shoes in the kitchen, she thought. I'll ruin my stockings out here.

"I take it he wasn't even a very good friend of yours," Mr. Benson said.

"You'd take it right." Because that sounded rude, she added quickly: "Nobody understands that. He was just a boy I knew."

"Shouldn't be so hard to understand."

"It's like a wake in there, and that's silly."

"Well," Mr.Benson said, "he was nineteen and maybe when it's somebody that young, you don't even have to know him to mourn after him."

"He was twenty." Susan looked at Mr. Benson then, the short stocky man, with a fringe of black hair around his ears and a sweaty pink skull shining in the heat. His eyes, buried in folds of puffy skin, were small points of blue. My father might have looked like that, she thought.

"Twenty's still pretty young," he said.

"This whole thing is my mother. The minute she saw the telegram all she could think of is how history is repeating itself. She's called everybody, even people she doesn't like."

"I know your mother," Mr. Benson said.

"And that dying in glory talk." Susan hopped off the railing and leaned against it, palms pressing the rough wood. "That's all I ever hear. My mother knows those stories—the ones you were telling on the porch—she knows it's awful and stupid and terrible."

"No," Mr. Benson said, "it isn't awful." He pulled a cigarette holder from his pocket and began to suck it. "I gave up smoking and this is all I got left...You're wrong, child, but maybe the stories don't say it clear enough."

Susan said slowly, "You talk about it all the time, any time."

He nodded slowly and the empty cigarette holder whistled in the hot afternoon air. "Because it was the most glorious thing ever happened to us."

"Too bad you can't tell Harold," she said.

"Take Harold now." Mr. Benson's voice was dull and monotonous, singsonging in the heat. "He didn't have to join up right out of high school. Draft calls been pretty low around here lately."

"He knew he was going to have to, that's why."

"It don't happen like that." He blew through the cigarette holder again, then tapped it on his palm. "Always seemed to me like men have got to have their war. I had to have mine twenty-five years ago. When you're in it maybe it's different, but you got to go. Once you hear about it, you got to go to it."

"That doesn't make any sense to me," Susan said. "None."

"Even when you're in it, you know that if you live, you're going to remember it all the rest of your life. And you know that if there was another war and you were young enough, you'd go again."

"That's stupid," Susan said.

"Maybe. You forget places you've been and you forget women you had, but you don't forget fighting."

Behind her the tea kettle gave a shriek. He glanced up. "Sounds like your water is boiling."

"Yes," she said, "I'll see to it."

He nodded and walked away, leaving a light smell of bourbon behind him. He turned once, lifted his hands, palms up in a little shrugging gesture.

She made her tea. As if she were obeying a set of rules. Things were beginning to feel less strange to her. Even the talk about Harold didn't seem as silly as it had.

I'm beginning not to mind, she thought, but it's still all mixed up. He was the sort of boy I could have married, but I didn't even know him. And that's lucky for me. Otherwise I might be like my mother. His being dead doesn't really change anything for me. I'll get married after a while to somebody as good as him or even better...

She drank her tea slowly; she was sad and happy at once. Harold was a young man who had died. He didn't leave a memory behind, he didn't leave anything. He was just gone and there wasn't even a mark at the place where he had been.

Her mother stood in the door. "Do you feel well enough to come back in, child?"

Susan chuckled, a quiet little self-contented chuckle.

"Whatever is funny, child?"

"You're having such a good time, Mother, you haven't had such a good time in ages."

"Well, really."

"You're alive and I'm alive and Harold's not alive."

"That's horrible."

"Sure."

She followed her mother across the waxed linoleum. "Wait, I've got to put my shoes on."

There just isn't anything, she thought. I'm sorry, Harold. I hope it wasn't too bad and I hope it didn't hurt too much. You and my father. I bet your parents have your picture on the mantel too.

Her shoes were on now and she straightened up.

"Good-by," she said in a very light whisper. "You poor bastard."

And she went inside to join the people.

Larry Heinemann
"The First Clean Fact"
1979

In 1966, at the age of 22, Larry Heinemann served in Vietnam as a combat infantryman with the 25th Division. Since then he has received literary fellowships from the Bread Loaf Writer's Conference, the National Endowment for the Arts and the Illinois Arts Council. His first novel is entitled Close Quarters. *"The First Clean Fact," originally published as a short story, is also the first chapter in Heinemann's most recent novel,* Paco's Story.

Let's begin with the first clean fact, James: This ain't no war story. War stories are out—one, two, three, and a heave-ho, into the lake you go with all the other alewife scuz and foamy harbor scum. But isn't it a pity. All those crinkly, soggy sorts of laid-by tellings crowded together as thick and pitiful as street cobbles, floating mushy bellies up, like so much moldy shag rug (dead as rusty-ass doornails and smelling so peculiar and un-Christian). Just isn't it a pity, because here and there and yonder among the corpses are some prize-winning, leg-pulling daisies—some real pop-in-the-oven muffins, so to speak, some real softly lobbed, easy-out line drives.

But that's the way of the world, or so the fairy tales go. The people with the purse strings and apron strings gripped in their hot and soft little hands denounce war stories—with perfect diction and practiced gestures—as a geek-monster species of evil-ugly rumor. (A geek, James, is a carnival performer whose whole act consists of biting the head off a live chicken or a snake.) These people who denounce war stories stand bolt upright and proclaim with broad and timely sweeps of the arm that war stories put *other* folks to sleep where they sit. (When the contrary is more to the truth, James. Any carny worth his cashbox—not dead or in jail or squirreled away in some county nuthouse—will tell you that most folks will shell out hard-earned, greenback cash, every time, to see artfully performed, urgently fascinating, grisly and gruesome carnage.)

Other people (getting witty and spry, floor-of-the-Senate, let-me-read-this-here-palaver-into--the *Congressional-Record,* showboat oratorical) slip one hand under a vest flap and slide one elegantly spit-shined wing-tip shoe forward ever so clever, and swear and be *damned* if all that snoring at war stories doesn't rattle windows for miles around—all the way to Pokorneyville, or so the papers claim. (Pokorneyville, James, is a real place, you understand, a little bit of a town between Wheeling and Half Day at the junction of U.S. Route 12 and Aptakisic Road—a Texaco gas station, a Swedish bakery, and Don't Drive Beddie-Bye Motel.)

And a distinct but mouthy minority—book-learned witch-craft amateurs and half-savvy street punks and patriots-for-cash (for some piddling hand-to-mouth wage, James)—slyly hang their heads and secretly insinuate that the snoring (he-honk, he-honk, the way a good, mean shake-shake-like-a-ragdoll snore snaps at you, James) is nothing if it isn't the Apocalypse itself choking on its own spit, trying to catch its breath for one more go-round.

And the geeks and freaks and sideshow drifters of this world hear the dipstick yokels soaking up a shill like that, well, damned if they don't haul off a belly laugh—haw haw haw. *They* know a prize-winning shuck when they hear one, James. They lean back in their folding lawn chairs, line up in front of their setups and shacks—the Skil-Thro and Ring Toss and Guess-How-Many-Pennies-in-the-Jar-Bub? and such as that—and slap their thighs hard enough to raise welts, all the while whispering among themselves that the rubs of this world will *never* get the hang of things.

Now, according to some people, folks do not want to hear about Alpha Company—us grunts—busting jungle and busting cherries from Landing Zone Skator-Gator to Scat Man Do (wherever *that* is), humping and *hauling ass* all the way. We used French Colonial maps back then—the names of towns and map symbols and elevation lines crinkled and curlicued and squeezed together, as incomprehensible as the Chiricahua dialect of Apache. We never could cipher a goddamned thing on those maps, so absolutely and precisely where Scat Man Do is tongue cannot tell, but we asked around and followed Lieutenant Stennett's nose—

flashing through some fine fire-fight possibilities, punji pits the size of copper mines, not to mention hog pens and chicken coops (scattering chickens and chicken feathers like so many wood chips). We made it to the fountain square in downtown Scat Man Do—and back to LZ Skator-Gator—in an afternoon, James, singing snatches of arias and duets from *Simon Boccanegra* and *The Flying Dutchman* at the top of our socks. But what we went there for no one every told us, and none of us—what was left of us that time—ever bothered to ask.

And some people think that folks do not want to hear about the night at Fire Base Sweet Pea when the Company got kicked in the mouth good and hard—street-fight hard—and wound up spitting slivers of brown teeth and bloody scabs for a fortnight. Lieutenant Stennett had us night-laagered in a lumpy, rocky slope down the way from high ground—his first (but by no stretch of your imagination his last) mistake. And you could hawk a gob of phlegm and spit into the woodline from your foxhole, James. And it was raining to beat the band. And no one was getting any sleep. And just after midnight—according to Gallagher's radium-dial watch—some zonked-out zip crawled up sneaky-close in the mangled underbrush and whispered in the pouring rain, "Hey, you! Rich-chard Nick-zun is a egg-suckin' hunk of runny owlshit!" And then Paco and the rest of us heard him and some other zip giggling—tee-hee-hee-hee—as though that was the world's worst thing they could think to say, and would provoke us into rageful anger. But before any of us could wipe the rain out of our eyes, Jonesy raised his head from his rucksack, where he was taking one of his famous naps—fucking the duck, we called it—and stage-whispered right back, "Listen, you squint-eyed spook, you ain' tellin' me annathang ah don' know!" Then they whispered back at us with one voice, as giggly and shivery cute as a couple smart-ass six-year-olds, "GI, you *die* tonight!" and then giggled some more. Paco blinked his eyes slowly, glancing out of the corners as if to say he didn't believe he heard what he *knew* he heard, and shook his head, saying out loud, "What do these zips think this is, some kind of chickenshit Bruce Dern—Michael J. Pollard—John Wayne movie? *"GI, you* die *tonight!'* What kind of a fucked-up attitude is that?" Then he leaned over his sopping-wet rucksack in the direction of the smirking giggles, put his hands to his mouth, megaphone-fashion, and said, "Hawkshit," loud enough for the whole company to hear. "Put your money where your mouth is, Slopehead," he said. "Whip it on me!" So later that night they did. They greased half the 4th platoon and Lieutenant Stennett's brand-new radioman, and we greased so many of them it wasn't even funny. The lieutenant got pissed off at Paco for mouthing off and getting his radioman blown away so soon—but that was okay, because the lieutenant wasn't "wrapped too tight," as Jonesy would say.

The next morning we got up, brushed ourselves off, cleared away the air-strike garbage—the firefight junk and jungle junk—and dusted off the walking wounded and the litter wounded and the body bags. And the morning after that, just as right as rain, James, we saddled up our rucksacks and slugged off into the deepest, baddest part of the Goongone Forest north of our base camp at Phuc Luc, looking to kick some ass—anybody's ass (can you dig it, James?)—and take some names. Yessiree! We hacked and humped our way from one end of that goddamned woods to the other—crisscrossing wherever our whim took us—no more sophisticated or complicated or elegant than an organized gang; looking to nail any and all of that goddamned giggling slime we came across to the barn door. Then one bright and cheery morning, when our month was up, Private First Class Elijah Raintree George Washington Carver Jones (Jonesy for short, James) had thirty-nine pairs of blackened, leathery, wrinkly ears strung on a bit of black commo wire and wrapped like a garland around that bit of turned-out brim of his steel helmet. He had snipped the ears off with a pearl-handled straight razor just as quick and slick as you'd lance a boil the size of a baseball—snicker-snack—the way he bragged his uncle could skin a poached deer. He cured the ears a couple days by tucking them under that bit of turned-out brim of his steel helmet, then toted them crammed in a spare sock. The night that Lieutenant Stennett called it quits, Jonesy sat up way after dark stringing those ears on that bit of black wire and sucking snips of C-ration beefsteak through his teeth.

And the next afternoon, when we finally humped through the south gate at Phuc Luc, you should have seen those rear-area motherfucking housecats bug their eyes and cringe every muscle in their bodies, and generally suck back against the buildings (you would have been right proud, James). Jonesy danced this way and that—shucking and jiving, juking and high-stepping, rolling his eyes and snapping his fingers in time—twirling that necklace to a fare-thee-well, shaking and jangling it (as much as a necklace of ears will jangle, James) and generally fooling with it as though it were a cheerleader's pom-pom.

And the Phuc Luc base camp Viets couldn't help but look, too. Now, the Viets worked the PX checkout counters (good-looking women who had to put out right smart and regular to keep their jobs), the PX barbershop (where the Viet barbers could run a thirty-five-cent haircut into $6.50 in fifteen minutes), and the stylishly thatched souvenir shack (where a bandy-legged ARVN cripple sold flimsy beer coolers and zip-a-dee-doo-dah housecat ashtrays, and athletic-style jackets that had a map embroidered on the back with the scrolled legend *Hot damn—Vietnam* sewn in underneath). And, James, don't you know they were Viets during the day and zips at night; one zip we body-counted one time couldn't booby-trap a shithouse any better than he could cut hair.

Every Viet in base camp crowded the doorways and screened windows, and such as that, gawking at Jonesy—and the rest of us, too. So he made a special show of shaking those ears at them, witch-doctor-fashion, while booming out some gibberish mumbo jumbo in his best amen-corner baritone and laughing that cool, nasty, grisly laugh of his, acting the jive fool for all those housecats. And the rest of the company—what was left of us *that* time—laughed at him, too, even though we humped those last three hundred meters to the tents (up an incline) on sloppy, bloody blisters, with our teeth gritted and the fraying rucksack straps squeezing permanent grooves in our shoulders. (A body never gets used to humping, James. When the word comes, you saddle your rucksack on your back, take a deep breath and set your jaw good and tight, then lean a little forward, as though you're walking into a stiff and blunt nor'easter, and begin by putting one foot in front of the other. After a good little while you've got two sharp pains as straight as a die from your shoulders to your kidneys, but there's nothing to do for it but grit your teeth a little harder and keep humping. And swear to God, James, those last uphill three hundred meters were the sorriest, goddamnedest three hundred motherfuckers in all of Southeast Asia. Captain Courtney Culpepper, who never missed a chance to flash his West Point class ring in your face—that ring the size of a Hamilton railroad watch— never once sent the trucks to meet us at the gate: said we had humped that far, might as well hump the rest.)

Nor do people think that folks want to hear what a stone bore (and we do mean *stone*, James) sitting bunker guard could be. Now some troopers called it perimeter guard and some called it berm guard, but it was all the same. The bunkers, James: broad, sloping sandbagged affairs the size of a forty-acre farm on the outside and a one-rack clothes closet inside, lined up every forty meters or so along the perimeter, within easy grenade range of the concertina wire and the marsh. You sit scrunched up, bent-backed, and stoop-shouldered on a plain pine plank, staring through a gun slit the size of a mail slot. And you stare at a couple hundred meters of shitty-ass marsh that no zip in his right mind would try to cross, terraced rice paddy long gone to seed, and a raggedy-assed, beat-to-shit woodline yonder. (That woodline was *all* fucked up, James, because we used to shoot it up every now and again out of sheer fucking boredom.) Well, you stare at all that, and stare at it, until the moonlit, starlit image of weeds and reeds and bamboo saplings and bubbling marsh slime burns itself into the back of your head in the manner of

Daguerre's first go with a camera obscura. You peep through that skinny-ass embrasure with your M-16 on full rock and roll, a double armful of fragmentation grenades—frags, we called them—hanging above your head on a double arm's length of tripflare wire, and every hour at the quarter hour you crank up the land-line handphone and call in a situation report—sit-rep, we called it—to the main bunker up the hill in back of you fifty paces or so. "Hell-o? Hell-o, Main Bunker!" you say, extra-friendly-like. "Yez," comes this sleepy, scrawny voice, mellowed by forty meters of land-line commo wire. "This here is Bunker Number 7," you say, and snatch one more glance downrange—everything bone-numb evil and cathedral-quiet. "Everything is okeydokey. Hunky-dory. In-the-pink and couldn't-be-sweeter!" And that sleepy, scrawny voice takes a good long pause, and takes a breath, and drawls right back at you, "Well, okay, cuz!"

And between those calls up the hill—and taking a break every now and again to take a whiz, downrange—you have nothing better to do than stare at that marsh and twiddle your thumbs and give the old pecker a few tugs for the practice, wet-dreaming about that Eurasian broad with the luscious, exquisite titties who toured with a Filipino trio and turned tricks for anyone of commissioned rank.

Those Filipinos, James, they were extra-ordinary. One guy played a rickety Hawaiian guitar, one guy played a banged-up tenor saxophone, and the third guy played the electric accordion—and that dude could squeeze some *fine* accordion, James. That trio and the woman played every nickel-and-dime base camp, every falling-down mess hall and sleazy, scruffy Enlisted Men's Club south of the 17th Parallel (the DMZ, we called)—as famous in their own way as Washing Machine Charlie, the legendary night rider of Guadalcanal. So how come they never made the papers, you may ask.

Well, James, reporters, as a gang, acted as though our whole purpose for being there was to entertain them. They'd look at you from under the snappily canted brim of an Abercrombie & Fitch Australian bush hat as much as to say, "Come on, kid, *astonish* me! Say *something* fucked up and quotable, *something* evil, something *bloody* and *nasty*, and be quick about it—I ain't got all day; I'm on a deadline." But mostly you'd see them with one foot on the lead-pipe rail and one elbow on the stained plywood bar of the Mark Twain Lounge of the Hyatt-Regency Saigon, swilling ice-cold raspberry daiquiris and vodka sours by the pitcherful—pussy drinks, bartenders call them. The younger, "hipper" ones popped opium on the sly or sprinkled it on their jays, and chewed speed like Aspergum, but their rap was the same, "Don't these ignorant fucking grunts *die* ugly! It's goddamned *bee-utiful!*" They'd lean side-ways against the bar, drugstore-cowboy-style—twiddling their swizzle sticks—and stare down at their rugged-looking L.L. Bean hiking boots or Adidas triple-stripe delux gym shoes, swapping bullshit lies and up-country war stories. "Say, Jack," would say this dried-up, milky-eyed old sports hack from the *Pokorneyville Weekly Volunteer-Register*, "I seen this goofy, wiggy-eyed, light-skinned spade up at Fire Base Gee-Gaw las' week. Had some weird shit scrawled on the back of his flak jacket, Jack: 'Rule 1. Take no shit. Rule 2. Cut no slack. Rule 3. Kill all prisoners.' I ast him if he was octoroon—he looked octoroon to me—and he says (can you beat this?), 'I ain't octoroon, I'm from Philly!' Haw-shit, buddy-boy, some of these nigras is awful D-U-M-B." Then slush-eyes'll take another couple he-man slugs of raspery daiquiri, smacking his lips and grinning to high heaven.

So, James, listening to conversation like that, how can anyone except reporters and journalists—and that kind—would appreciate anything as subtle and arcane and pitiful as one three-piece USO band and the snazziest, hot-to-trot honey-fuck to hit the mainland since the first French settlers. Those guys can't be everywhere, now, can they?

Those Filipinos ha-wonked and razza-razzed and pee-winged, sharping and flatting right along for close to three hours down at the lighted end of our company mess hall. The whole charm of their music was the fact that they couldn't hit the same note at the same time at the same pitch if you passed a hat, plunked the money down, put a .45 to their heads, and said, "There! Now, damnit, play!" They played the "Orange Blossom Special" and "Home on the Range" and "You Ain't Nothing but a Hound Dog" and "I Can't Get No Satisfaction," after a fashion. And they played songs like "Good Night, Irene" and "I Wonder Who's Kissing Her Now" and "I Love You a Bushel and a Peck"—music nobody ever heard of but the gray-headed lifers. And that woman, who hardly had a stitch on (and she was one fluffy dish, James), wiggled pretty little titties right in the colonel's mustache—Colonel Hubbel having himself a front-row kitchen chair—and she sure did sit him up straight, *all right*. And the rest of the battalion officers and hangers-on (artillery chaplains and brigade headquarters busy-bodies on the slum) sat shoulder patch to shoulder patch in a squared-off semicircle just as parade-ground pretty as you please. They crossed their legs to hide their hard-ons, and tried to look as blasé and matter-of-fact—as officer-like and gentlemanly—as was possible, trying to keep us huns away from the honey. And the rest of the company, us grunts, stood close-packed on the floor and the chairs and tables, and hung, one-armed, from the rafters—our tongues hanging out, swilling beer from the meat locker and circle-jerking our brains out. Our forearms just a-flying, James; our forearms just a blur. And that broad shimmied and pranced around near-naked, jiggling her sweating little titties like someone juggling two one-pound lumps of greasy, shining hamburger, and dry-humping the air with sure and steady rhythmic thrusts of her nifty little snatch—ta-tada-ha-humpa, ta-tada-ha-humpa, ta-tada-ha-humpa, *ha-whoo*! Then a couple of black guys from the 3rd platoon's ambush began to clap their hands in time and shout, "Come awn, Sweet Pea, twiddle those goddamn thangs in my mustache! Come awn, Coozie, why don't ya'll sit awn *my* face—yaw haw haw."

(Let's tell it true, James, do you expect we'll ever see that scene in a movie?)

But most particularly, people think that folks do not want to hear about the night at Fire Base Harriette—down the way from LZ Skator-Gator, and within earshot of a ragtag bunch of mud-and-thatch hooches everyone called Gookville—when the whole company, except for one guy, got killed. Fucked-up dead, James; scarfed up. Everybody but Paco got nominated and voted into the Hall of Fame in one fell swoop. The company was night-laagered in a tight-assed perimeter up past our eyeballs in a no-shit firefight with a battalion of headhunter NVA—corpses and cartridge brass and oily magazines and dud frags scattered around, and everyone running low on ammo. Lieutenant Stennett crouched over his radio hoarsely screaming map coordinates to every piece of artillery, every air strike and gunship within radio range, like it was going out of style, when all of a sudden—*zoom*—the air came alive and crawled and yammered and whizzed and hummed with the roar and buzz of a thousand incoming rounds. It was hard to see for all the gunpowder smoke and dust kicked up by all the muzzle flashes, but everyone looked up—GIs *and* zips—and knew it was every incoming round left in Creation, a wild and bloody shitstorm, a ball-busting cataclysm. We knew that the dirt under our bellies (and the woods and the villes and us with it) was going to be pulverized to ash and we do mean *pulverized*, James), so you could draw a thatch rake through it and not find the chunks; knew by the overwhelming, ear-piercing whine we swore was splitting our heads wide open that those rounds were the size of houses. We don't know what the rest of the company did, or the zips for that matter, but the 2nd squad of the 2nd platoon swapped that peculiar look around that travels from victim to victim in any disaster. We ciphered it out right then and there that we couldn't dig a hole deep enough, fast enough; couldn't crawl under something thick enough; couldn't drop our rifles, and whatnot, and turn tail and beat feet far enough but that this incoming wouldn't catch us by the scruff of the shirt, so to speak, and lay us lengthwise. We looked round at one another as much to say, *"Oh fuck!* My man, this ain't your average, ordinary, everyday, garden-variety sort of incoming. This one's going to blow everybody down." Swear to God, James, there are those days—no matter how hard you hump and scrap and scratch—when there is simply nothing left to do but pucker and submit. Paco slipped off his bandanna and sprinkled the last of his canteen water on it, wiped his face and hands, then twirled it up again and tied it around his neck—the knot to one side. Jonesy laid himself out, with his head on his rucksack, getting ready to take another one of his famous naps. Most of the rest of us simply sat back and ran our fingers through our hair to make ourselves as presentable as possible. And Gallagher, who had a red-and-black tattoo of a dragon on his forearm from his wrist to his elbow, buttoned his shirt sleeves and brushed himself off, and sat cross-legged, with his hands folded meditatively in his lap. In another instant everyone within earshot was quiet, and a hush of anticipation rippled through the crowd, like a big wind that strikes many trees all at once. Then we heard the air rushing ahead of those rounds the same as a breeze through a cave—so sharp and cool on the face, refreshing and foul all at once—as though those rounds were floating down to us as limp and leisurely as cottonwood leaves. We looked one another up and down one more time, as much as to say, "Been nice. See you around. *Fucking shit*! Here it comes."

And in less time than it takes to tell it, James, we screamed loud and nasty, and everything was transformed into Crispy Critters for half a dozen clicks in any direction you would have cared to point; everything smelling of ash and marrow and spontaneous combustion; everything—dog tags, slivers of meat, letters from home, scraps of sandbags and rucksacks and MPC scrip, jungle shit and human shit—*everything* hanging out of the woodline looking like so much rust-colored puke.

Yes, sir, James, we screamed our gonads slam-up, squeeze-up against our diaphragms, screamed volumes of unprintable oaths. When the motherfuckers hit we didn't go *poof* of a piece; rather, we disappeared like sand dunes in a stiff and steady offshore ocean breeze—one goddamned grain at a time. We disappeared the same as if someone had dropped a spot of dirt into a tall, clear glass of water—bits of mud trailed behind that spot until it finally dissolved and nothing reached bottom but a swirling film. (Not that it didn't smart, James. O, it tickled right smart. First it thumped ever so softly on the top of our heads—your fat-assed uncle patting you on your hat, leaning way back and bragging his fool head off about how proud he is of the way you do your chores. But then came the bone-crushing, ball-busting rush—the senior class's butter-headed peckerwood flashing around the locker room, snapping the trademark corner of a sopping-wet shower towel upside everyone's head with a might crack. Whack!)

Whooie! We reared back and let her rip so loud and vicious that all the brothers and sisters at Parson Doo-dah's Meeting House Revival fled—we mean *split*, James; we mean they peeled the varnish off the double front doors in their haste. The good parson was stalking back and forth in front of the pulpit rail, shouting and getting happy, slapping his big meaty hands together, signifying those sinners—bim-bam-boom— and calling on the mercy of Sweet Jesus. Well, sir, our screams hit the roofing tin like the dictionary definition of a hailstorm and swooped down the coal-stove chimney—*"Ah-shoo!"* Those sinners jumped back a row or two as though Brother Doo-dah had thrown something scalding in their faces. They threw up their arms, wiggle and wagged their fingers, shouting to high heaven, "Alle-lujah!" "A-men!" "Yes, Lord!" "Save me, Jesus!" Then they grabbed their dog-eared Bibles and hand-crocheted heirloom shawls, and hit the bricks. Yes, sir, James, plenty of the good brothers and sisters got right and righteous *that* night. And Brother Doo-dah was left standing in the settling dust slowly scratching his bald, shining head, pondering—wondering—just exactly how did he do that marvelous thing?

Oh, we dissolved all right, everybody but Paco, but our screams burst through the ozone; burst through the rags and tatters and cafe-curtain-looking aurora borealis, and so forth and suchlike; clean as a whistle; clean as a new car—unfucked-with and frequency-perfect out into God's Everlasting Cosmos. Out where it's hot enough to shrivel your eyeballs to the shape and color and consistency of raisins; out where it's cold enough to freeze your breath to resemble slab plastic.

And we're pushing up daisies for half a handful of millennia (we're *all* pushing up daisies, James), until we're powder fine than talc, *finer* than fine, as smooth and hollow as an old salt lick—but that blood-curdling scream is rattling all over God's ever-loving Creation like a BB in a boxcar, only louder.

Tobias Wolff
"Wingfield"
1981

Tobias Wolff spent four years in the army in the paratroops. In Vietnam, 1967-1968, he served as an adviser to the Vietnamese 7th Infantry Division in the Mekong Delta. Wolff teaches at Syracuse University and publishes his fiction in Esquire, Vanity Fair, The Atlantic, *and many other magazines. In 1985 he won the PEN/Faulkner Award for his short novel* The Barracks Thief. *Collections of his stories include* In the Garden of the North American Martyrs *and* Back in the World.

When we arrived at the camp, they pulled us off the buses and made us do push-ups in the parking lot. The asphalt was hot and tar stuck to our noses. They made fun of our clothes and took them away from us. They shaved our heads until little white scars showed through, then filled our arms with boots and belts and helmets and punctured them with needles.

In the middle of the night they came to our barracks and walked up and down between us as we stood by our bunks. They looked at us. If we looked at them they said, "Why are you looking at me?" and made us do push-ups. If you didn't act right they made your life sad.

They divided us into companies, platoons, and squads. In my squad were Wingfield and Parker and seven others. Parker was a wise guy, my friend. I never saw anything get him down except malaria. Wingfield, before the military took responsibility for him, had been kept alive somewhere in North Carolina. When he was in a condition to talk his voice oozed out of him thick and slow and sweet. His eyes when he had them open were the palest blue. Most of the time they were closed.

He often fell asleep while he polished his boots, and once while he was shaving. They ordered him to paint baseboards and he curled up in the corner and let the baseboards take care of themselves. They found him with his head resting on his outstretched arm, his mouth open; a string of paint had dried between the brush and the floor.

In the afternoons they showed us films: from these we learned how to maintain our jeeps, how to protect our teeth from decay, how to treat foreigners, and how to sheathe ourselves against boils, nervous disorders, madness, and finally the long night of the blind. The foreigners wore shiny suits and carried briefcases. They smiled as they directed our soldiers to their destinations. They would do the same for us if we could remember how to ask them questions. As we repeated the important phrases to ourselves we could hear the air whistling in and out of Wingfield's mouth, rattling in the depths of his throat.

Wingfield slept as they showed us how our weapons worked, and what plants we could browse on if we got lost or ran out of food. Sometimes they caught him and made him stand up; he would smile shyly, like a young girl, and find something to lean against, and go back to sleep. He slept while we marched, which other soldiers could do; but other soldiers marched straight when they were supposed to turn and turned when they were supposed to march straight. They marched into trees and ditches and walls, they fell into holes. Wingfield could march around corners while asleep. He could sing the cadence and double-time at port arms without opening his eyes. You had to see it to believe it.

At the end of our training they drove us deep into the woods and set our company against another. To make the numbers even they gave the other side six of our men, Wingfield among them. He did not want to go but they made him. Then they handed out blank ammunition and colored scarves, blue for us and red for them.

The presence of these two colors made the woods dangerous. We tiptoed from bush to bush, crawled on our stomachs through brown needles under the stunted pines. The bark of the trees was sweating amber resin but you couldn't stop and stare. If you dawdled and daydreamed you would be taken in ambush. When soldiers with red scarves walked by we hid and shot them from behind and sent them to the parking lot, which was no longer a parking lot but the land of the dead.

A wind sprang up, bending and shaking the trees; their shadows lunged at us. Then darkness fell over the woods, sudden as a trap closing. Here and there we saw a stab of flame and heard a shot, but soon this scattered firing fell away. We pitched tents and posted guards; sat in silence and ate food from cans, cold. Our heartbeats echoed in our helmets.

Parker threw rocks. We heard them thumping the earth, breaking brittle branches as they fell. Someone yelled at him to stop, and Parker pointed where the shout came from.

Then we blackened our faces and taped our jingling dog tags, readied ourselves to raid. We slipped into the darkness as though we belonged there, like shadows. Gnats swarmed, mosquitos stung us but we did not slap; we were that stealthy. We went on until we saw, not far ahead, a fire. A fire! The fools had made a fire! Parker put his hand over his mouth and shook his head from side to side, signifying laughter. The rest of us did the same.

We only had to find the guards to take the camp by surprise. I found one right away, mumbling and exclaiming in his sleep, his rifle propped against a tree. It was Wingfield. With hatred and contempt and joy I took him from behind, and as I drew it across his throat I was wishing that my finger was a knife. Twisting in my arms, he looked into my black face and said, "Oh my God," as though I was no imposter but Death himself.

Then we stormed the camp, firing into the figures lumped in the sleeping bags, firing into the tents and into the shocked white faces at the tent flaps. It was exactly the same thing that happened to us a year and three months later as we slept beside a canal in the Mekong Delta, a few kilometers from Ben Tre.

We were sent home on leave when our training ended, and when we regrouped, several of us were missing, sick or AWOL or sent overseas to fill the ranks of units picked clean in the latest fighting. Wingfield was among them. I never saw him again and I never expected to. From now on his nights would be filled with shadows like me, and against such enemies what chance did Wingfield have?

Parker got malaria two weeks before the canal attack, and was still in the hospital when it happened. When he got out they sent him to another unit. He wrote letters to me but I never answered them. They were full of messages for people who weren't alive any more, and I thought it would be a good thing if he never knew this. Then he would lose only one friend instead of twenty-six. At last the letters stopped and I did not hear from him again for nine years, when he knocked on my door one evening just after I'd come home from work.

He had written my parents, he explained, and they had told him where I was living. He said that he and his wife and daughter were just passing through on their way to Canada, but I knew better. There were other ways to go than this and travelers always took them. He wanted an accounting.

Parker's daughter played with my dogs and his wife cooked steaks in the barbecue pit while we drank beer and talked and looked each other over. He was still cheerful, but in a softer, slower way, like a jovial uncle of the boy he'd been. After we ate we lay on the blanket until the bugs got to our ankles and the child began to whine. Parker's wife carried the dishes into the house and washed them while we settled on the steps. The light from the kitchen window laid a garish patch upon the lawn. Things crawled toward it under the grass. Parker asked the question he'd come to ask and then sat back and waited while I spoke name after name into the night. When I finished he said, "Is that all? What about Washington?"

"I told you. He got home all right."

"You're sure about that?"

"Of course I'm sure."

"You ought to get married," Parker said, standing up. "You take yourself too seriously. What the hell, right?"

Parker's daughter was lying on the living-room floor next to my golden retriever, who growled softly in his sleep as Parker lifted the girl and slung her over his shoulder. His wife took my arm and leaned against me as we walked out to the car. "I feel so comfortable with you," she said. "You remind me of my grandfather."

"By the way," Parker said, "do you remember Wingfield?"

"He was with that first bunch that got sent over," I said. "I don't think he made it back."

"Who told you that?"

"Nobody. I just don't think he did."

"You're wrong. I saw him." Parker shifted the girl to his other shoulder. "That's what I was going to tell you. I was in Charlotte six months ago and I saw him in the train station, sitting on a bench."

"You didn't."

"Oh yes I did."

"How was he? What did he say?"

"He didn't say anything. I was in a hurry and he looked so peaceful I just couldn't bring myself to wake him up."

"But it was definitely him?"

"It was Wingfield all right. He had his mouth open."

I waved at their car until it made the turn at the end of the street. Then I rummaged through the garbage and filled the dogs' bowls with the bones and gristle Parker's wife had thrown away. As I inspected the dishes she had washed the thought came to me that this was a fussy kind of thing for a young man to do.

I opened a bottle of wine and went outside. The coals in the cooking pit hissed and flushed as the wind played over them, pulling away the smoke in tight spirals. I sensed the wings of the bats above me, wheeling in the darkness. Like a soldier on leave, like a boy who knows nothing at all, like a careless and go-to-hell fellow I drank to them. Then I drank to the crickets and locusts and cicadas who purred so loudly that the earth itself seemed to be snoring. I drank to the snoring earth, to the closed eye of the moon, to the trees that nodded and sighed: until, already dreaming, I fell back upon the blanket.

Tim O'Brien
"The Things They Carried"
1986

Tim O'Brien was born in rural Minnesota in 1947. Drafted in 1968, he served two years as an infantryman in Vietnam. His books include If I Die in a Combat Zone; Northern Lights; Going After Cacciato, *which won the National Book Award in 1979; and his most recent novel,* The Nuclear Age. *His stories appear in the* O. Henry Prize *and* Best American Short Stories *collections, and he has been the recipient of both Guggenheim and National Endowment for the Arts fellowships in prose.*

First Lieutenant Jimmy Cross carried letters from a girl named Martha, a junior at Mount Sebastian College in New Jersey. They were not love letters, but Lieutenant Cross was hoping, so he kept them folded in plastic at the bottom of his rucksack. In the late afternoon, after a day's march, he would dig his foxhole, wash his hands under a canteen, unwrap the letters, hold them with the tips of his fingers, and spend the last hour of light pretending. He would imagine romantic camping trips into the White Mountains in New Hampshire. He would sometimes taste the envelope flaps, knowing her tongue had been there. More than anything, he wanted Martha to love him as he loved her, but the letters were mostly chatty, elusive on the matter of love. She was a virgin, he was almost sure. She was an English major at Mount Sebastian, and she wrote beautifully about her professors and roommates and midterm exams, about her respect for Chaucer and her great affection for Virginia Woolf. She often quoted lines of poetry; she never mentioned the war, except to say, Jimmy, take care of yourself. The letters weighed ten ounces. They were signed "Love, Martha," but Lieutenant Cross understood that Love was only a way of signing and did not mean what he sometimes pretended it meant. At dusk, he would carefully return the letters to his rucksack. Slowly, a bit distracted, he would get up and move among his men, checking the perimeter, then at full dark he would return to his hole and watch the night and wonder if Martha was a virgin.

The things they carried were largely determined by necessity. Among the necessities or near-necessities were P-38 can openers, pocket knives, heat tabs, wrist watches, dog tags, mosquito repellent, chewing gum, candy, cigarettes, salt tablets, packets of Kool-Aid, lighters, matches, sewing kits, Military Payment Certificates, C rations, and two or three canteens of water. Together, these items weighed between fifteen and twenty pounds, depending upon a man's habits or rate of metabolism. Henry Dobbins, who was a big man, carried extra rations; he was especially fond of canned peaches in heavy syrup over pound cake. Dave Jensen, who practiced field hygiene, carried a toothbrush, dental floss, and several hotel-size bars of soap he'd stolen on R&R in Sydney, Australia. Ted Lavender, who was scared, carried tranquilizers until he was shot in the head outside the village of Than Khe in mid-April. By necessity, and because it was SOP, they all carried steel helmets that weighed five pounds including the liner and camouflage cover. They carried the standard fatigue jackets and trousers. Very few carried underwear. On their feet they carried jungle boots—2.1 pounds—and Dave Jensen carried three pairs of socks and a can of Dr. Scholl's foot powder as a precaution against trench foot. Until he was shot, Ted Lavender carried six or seven ounces of premium dope, which for him was a necessity. Mitchell Sanders, the RTO, carried condoms. Norman Bowker carried a diary. Rat Kiley carried comic books. Kiowa, a devout Baptist, carried an illustrated New Testament that had been presented to him by his father, who taught Sunday school in Oklahoma City, Oklahoma. As a hedge against bad times, however, Kiowa also carried his grandmother's distrust of the white man, his grandfather's old hunting hatchet. Necessity dictated. Because the land was mined and booby-trapped, it was SOP for each man to carry a steel-centered, nylon-covered flak jacket, which weighted 6.7 pounds, but which on hot days seemed much heavier. Because you could die so quickly, each man carried at least one large compress bandage, usually in the helmet band for easy access. Because the nights were cold, and because the monsoons were wet, each carried a green plastic poncho that could be used as a raincoat or groundsheet or makeshift tent. With its quilted liner, the poncho weighed almost two pounds, but it was worth every ounce. In April, for instance, when Ted Lavender was shot, they used his poncho to wrap him up, then to carry him across the paddy, then to lift him into the chopper that took him away.

They were called legs or grunts.

To carry something was to "hump" it, as when Lieutenant Jimmy Cross humped his love for Martha up the hills and through the swamps. In its intransitive form, "to hump" meant "to walk," or "to march," but it implied burdens far beyond the intransitive.

Almost everyone humped photographs. In his wallet, Lieutenant Cross carried two photographs of Martha. The first was a Kodachrome snapshot signed "Love," though he knew better. She stood against a brick wall. Her eyes were gray and neutral, her lips slightly open as she stared straight-on at the camera. At night, sometimes, Lieutenant Cross wondered who had taken the picture, because he knew she had boyfriends, because he loved her so much, and because he could see the shadow of the picture taker spreading out against the brick wall. The second photograph had been clipped from the 1968 Mount Sebastian yearbook. It was an action shot—women's volleyball—and Martha was bent horizontal to the floor, reaching, the palms of her hands in sharp focus, the tongue taut, the expression frank and competitive. There was no visible sweat. She wore white gym shorts. Her legs, he thought, were almost certainly the legs of a virgin, dry and without hair, the left knee cocked and carrying her entire weight, which was just over one hundred pounds. Lieutenant Cross remembered touching that left knee. A dark theater, he remembered, and the movie was *Bonnie and Clyde*, and Martha wore a tweed skirt, and during the final scene, when he touched her knee, she turned and looked at him in a sad, sober way that made him pull his hand back, but he would always remember the feel of the tweed skirt and the knee beneath it and the sound of the gunfire that killed

Bonnie and Clyde, how embarrassing it was, how slow and oppressive. He remembered kissing her goodnight at the dorm door. Right then, he thought, he should've done something brave. He should've carried her up the stairs to her room and tied her to the bed and touched that left knee all night long. He should've risked it. Whenever he looked at the photographs, he thought of new things he should've done.

What they carried was partly a function of rank, partly of field specialty.

As a first lieutenant and platoon leader, Jimmy Cross carried a compass, maps, code books, binoculars, and a .45-caliber pistol that weighed 2.9 pounds fully loaded. He carried a strobe light and the responsibility for the lives of his men.

As an RTO, Mitchell Sanders carried the PRC-25 radio, a killer, twenty-six pounds with its battery.

As a medic, Rat Kiley carried a canvas satchel filled with morphine and plasma and malaria tablets and surgical tape and comic books and all the things a medic must carry, including M&M's for especially bad wounds, for a total weight of nearly twenty pounds.

As a big man, therefore a machine gunner, Henry Dobbins carried the M-60, which weighted twenty-three pounds unloaded, but which was almost always loaded. In addition, Dobbins carried between ten and fifteen pounds of ammunition draped in belts across his chest and shoulders.

As PFCs or Spec 4s, most of them were common grunts and carried the standard M-16 gas-operated assault rifle. The weapon weighed 7.5 pounds unloaded, 8.2 pounds with its full twenty-round magazine. Depending on numerous factors, such as topography and psychology, the riflemen carried anywhere from twelve to twenty magazines, usually in cloth bandoliers, adding on another 8.4 pounds at minimum, fourteen pounds at maximum. When it was available, they also carried M-16 maintenance gear—rods and steel brushes and swabs and tubes of LSA oil—all of which weighed about a pound. Among the grunts, some carried the M-79 grenade launcher, 5.9 pounds unloaded, a reasonably light weapon except for the ammunition, which was heavy. A single round weighed ten ounces. The typical load was twenty-five rounds. But Ted Lavender, who was scared, carried thirty-four rounds when he was shot and killed outside Than Khe, and he went down under an exceptional burden, more than twenty pounds of ammunition, plus the flak jacket and helmet and rations and water and toilet paper and tranquilizers and all the rest, plus the unweighed fear. He was dead weight. There was no twitching or flopping. Kiowa, who saw it happen, said it was like watching a rock fall, or a big sandbag or something—just boom, then down—not like the movies where the dead guy rolls around and does fancy spins and goes ass over teakettle—not like that, Kiowa said, the poor bastard just flat-fuck fell. Boom. Down. Nothing else. It was a bright morning in mid-April. Lieutenant Cross felt the pain. He blamed himself. They stripped off Lavender's canteens and ammo, all the heavy things, and Rat Kiley said the obvious, the guy's dead, and Mitchell Sanders used his radio to report one U.S. KIA and to request a chopper. Then they wrapped Lavender in his poncho. They carried him out to a dry paddy, established security, and sat smoking the dead man's dope until the chopper came. Lieutenant Cross kept to himself. He pictured Martha's smooth young face, thinking he loved her more than anything, more than his men, and now Ted Lavender was dead because he loved her so much and could not stop thinking about her. When the dust-off arrived, they carried Lavender aboard. Afterward they burned Than Khe. They marched until dusk, then dug their holes, and that night Kiowa kept explaining how you had to be there, how fast it was, how the poor guy just dropped like so much concrete. Boom-down, he said. Like cement.

In addition to the three standard weapons—the M-60, M-16, and M-79—they carried whatever presented itself, or whatever seemed appropriate as a means of killing or staying alive. They carried catch-as-catch-can. At various times, in various situations, they carried M-14s and CAR-15s and Swedish Ks and grease guns and captured AK-47s and Chi-Coms and RPGs and Simonov carbines and black-market Uzis and .38-caliber Smith & Wesson handguns and 66 mm LAWs and shotguns and silencers and blackjacks and bayonets and C-4 plastic explosives. Lee Strunk carried a slingshot; a weapon of last resort, he called it. Mitchell Sanders carried brass knuckles. Kiowa carried his grandfather's feathered hatchet. Every third or fourth man carried a Claymore antipersonnel mine—3.5 pounds with its firing device. They all carried fragmentation grenades—fourteen ounces each. They all carried at least one M-18 colored smoke grenade—twenty-four ounces. Some carried CS or teargas grenades. Some carried white-phosphorus grenades. They carried all they could bear, and then some, including a silent awe for the terrible power of the things they carried.

In the first week of April, before Lavender died, Lieutenant Jimmy Cross received a good-luck charm from Martha. It was a simple pebble, an ounce at most. Smooth to the touch, it was a milky-white color with flecks of orange and violet, oval-shaped, like a miniature egg. In the accompanying letter, Martha wrote that she had found the pebble on the Jersey shoreline, precisely where the land touched water at high tide, where things came together but also separated. It was this separate-but-together quality, she wrote, that had inspired her to pick up the pebble and to carry it in her breast pocket for several days, where it seemed weightless, and then to send it through the mail, by air, as a token of her truest feelings for him. Lieutenant Cross found this romantic. But he wondered what her truest feelings were, exactly, and what she meant by separate-but-together. He wondered how the tides and waves had come into play on that afternoon along the Jersey shoreline when Martha saw the pebble and bent down to rescue it from geology. He imagined bare feet. Martha was a poet, with the poet's sensibilities, and her feet would be brown and bare, the toenails unpainted, the eyes chilly and somber like the ocean in March, and though it was painful, he wondered who had been with her that afternoon. He imagined a pair of shadows moving along the strip of sand where things came together but also separated. It was phantom jealousy, he knew, but he couldn't help himself. He loved her so much. On the march, through the hot days of early April, he carried the pebble in his mouth, turning it with his tongue, tasting sea salts and moisture. His mind wandered. He had difficulty keeping his attention on the war. On occasion he would yell at his men to spread out the column, to keep their eyes open, but then he would slip away into daydreams, just pretending, walking barefoot along the Jersey shore, with Martha, carrying nothing. He could feel himself rising. Sun and waves and gentle winds, all love and lightness.

What they carried varied by mission.

When a mission took them to the mountains, they carried mosquito netting, machetes, canvas tarps, and extra bug juice.

If a mission seemed especially hazardous, or if it involved a place they knew to be bad, they carried everything they could. In certain heavily mined AOs, where the land was dense with Toe Poppers and Bouncing Betties, they took turns humping a twenty-eight-pound mine detector. With its headphones and big sensing plate, the equipment was a stress on the lower back and shoulders, awkward to handle, often useless because of the shrapnel in the earth, but they carried it anyway, partly for safety, partly for the illusion of safety.

On ambush, or other night missions, they carried peculiar little odds and ends. Kiowa always took along his New Testament and a pair of moccasins for silence. Dave Jensen carried night-sight vitamins high in carotin. Lee Strunk carried his slingshot; ammo, he claimed, should never be a problem. Rat Kiley carried brandy and M&M's. Until he was shot, Ted Lavender carried the starlight scope, which weighed 6.3 pounds with its aluminum carrying case. Henry Dobbins carried his girlfriend's panty hose wrapped around his neck as a comforter. They all carried ghosts. When dark came, they would move out single file across the meadows and paddies to their ambush coordinates, where they would quietly set up the Claymores and lie down and spend the night waiting.

Other missions were more complicated and required special equipment. In mid-April, it was their mission to search out and destroy the elaborate tunnel complexes in the Than Khe area south of Chu Lai. To blow the tunnels, they carried one-pound blocks of pentrite high explosives, four blocks to a man, sixty-eight pounds in all. They carried wiring, detonators, and battery-powered clackers. Dave Jensen carried earplugs. Most often, before blowing the tunnels, they were ordered by higher command to search them, which was considered bad news, but by and large they just shrugged and carried out orders. Because he was a big man, Henry Dobbins was excused from tunnel duty. The others would draw numbers. Before Lavender died there were seventeen men in the platoon, and whoever drew the number seventeen would strip off his gear and crawl in headfirst with a flashlight and Lieutenant Cross's .45-caliber pistol. The rest of them would fan out as security. They would sit down or kneel, not facing the hole, listening to the ground beneath them, imagining cobwebs and ghosts, whatever was down there—the tunnel walls squeezing in—how the flashlight seemed impossibly heavy in the hand and how it was tunnel vision in the very strictest sense, compression in all ways, even time, and how you had to wiggle in— ass and elbows—a swallowed-up feeling—and how you found yourself worrying about odd things—will your flashlight go dead? Do rats carry rabies? If you screamed, how far would the sound carry? Would your buddies hear it? Would they have the courage to drag you out? In some respects, though not many, the waiting was worse than the tunnel itself. Imagination was a killer.

On April 16, when Lee Strunk drew the number seventeen, he laughed and muttered something and went down quickly. The morning was hot and very still. Not good, Kiowa said. He looked at the tunnel opening, then, out across a dry paddy toward the village of Than Khe. Nothing moved. No clouds or birds or people. As they waited, the men smoked and drank Kool-Aid, not talking much, feeling sympathy for Lee Strunk but also feeling the luck of the draw. You win some, you lose some, said Mitchell Sanders, and sometimes you settle for a rain check. It was a tired line and no one laughed.

Henry Dobbins ate a tropical chocolate bar. Ted Lavender popped a tranquilizer and went off to pee.

After five minutes, Lieutenant Jimmy Cross moved to the tunnel, leaned down, and examined the darkness. Trouble, he thought—a cave-in maybe. And then suddenly, without willing it, he was thinking about Martha. The stresses and fractures, the quick collapse, the two of them buried alive under all that weight. Dense, crushing love. Kneeling, watching the hole, he tried to concentrate on Lee Strunk and the war, all the dangers, but his love was too much for him, he felt paralyzed, he wanted to sleep inside her lungs and breathe her blood and be smothered. He wanted her to be a virgin and not a virgin, all at once. He wanted to know her. Intimate secrets—why poetry? Why so sad? Why that grayness in her eyes? Why so alone? Not lonely, just alone—riding her bike across campus or sitting off by herself in the cafeteria. Even dancing, she danced alone—and it was the aloneness that filled him with love. He remembered telling her that one evening. How she nodded and looked away. And how, later, when he kissed her, she received the kiss without returning it, her eyes wide open, not afraid, not a virgin's eyes, just flat and uninvolved.

Lieutenant Cross gazed at the tunnel. But he was not there. He was buried with Martha under the white sand at the Jersey shore. They were pressed together, and the pebble in his mouth was her tongue. He was smiling. Vaguely, he was aware of how quiet the day was, the sullen paddies, yet he could not bring himself to worry about matters of security. He was beyond that. He was just a kid at war, in love. He was twenty-two years old. He couldn't help it.

A few moments later Lee Strunk crawled out of the tunnel. He came up grinning, filthy but alive. Lieutenant Cross nodded and closed his eyes while the others clapped Strunk on the back and made jokes about rising from the dead.

Worms, Rat Kiley said. Right of the grave. Fuckin' zombie.

The men laughed. They all felt great relief.

Spook City, said Mitchell Sanders.

Lee Strunk made a funny ghost sound, a kind of moaning, yet very happy, and right then, when Strunk made that high happy moaning sound, when he went *Ahhooooo*, right then Ted Lavender was shot in the head on his way back from peeing. He lay with his mouth open. The teeth were broken. There was a swollen black bruise under his left eye. The cheekbone was gone. Oh shit, Rat Kiley said, the guy's dead. The guy's dead, he kept saying which seemed profound—the guy's dead. I mean really.

The things they carried were determined to some extent by superstition. Lieutenant Cross carried his good-luck pebble. Dave Jensen carried a rabbit's foot. Norman Bowker, otherwise a very gentle person, carried a thumb that had been presented to him as a gift by Mitchell Sanders. The thumb was dark brown, rubbery to the touch, and weighed four ounces at most. It had been cut from a VC corpse, a boy of fifteen or sixteen. They'd found him at the bottom of an irrigation ditch, badly burned, flies in his mouth and eyes. The boy wore black shorts and sandals. At the time of his death he had been carrying a pouch of rice, a rifle, and three magazines of ammunition.

You want my opinion, Mitchell Sanders said, there's a definite moral here.

He put his hand on the dead boy's wrist. He was quiet for a time, as if counting a pulse, then he patted the stomach, almost affectionately, and used Kiowa's hunting hatchet to remove the thumb.

Henry Dobbins asked what the moral was.

Moral?

You know. *Moral*

Sanders wrapped the thumb in toilet paper and handed it across to Norman Bowker. There was no blood. Smiling, he kicked the boy's head, watched the flies scatter, and said, It's like that old TV show—Paladin. Have gun, will travel.

Henry Dobbins thought about it.

Yeah, well, he finally said. I don't see no moral.

There it *is*, man.

Fuck off.

They carried USO stationery and pencils and pens. They carried Sterno, safety pins, trip flares, signal flares, spools of wire, razor blades, chewing tobacco, liberated joss sticks and statuettes of the smiling Buddha, candles, grease pencils, *The Stars and Stripes*, fingernail clippers, Psy Ops leaflets, bush hats, bolos, and much more. Twice a week, when the resupply choppers came in, they carried hot chow in green Mermite cans and large canvas bags filled with iced beer and soda pop. They carried plastic water containers, each with a two-gallon capacity. Mitchell Sanders carried a set of starched tiger fatigues for special occasions. Henry Dobbins carried Black Flag insecticide. Dave Jensen carried empty sandbags that could be filled at night for added protection. Lee Strunk carried tanning lotion. Some things they carried in common. Taking turns, they carried the big PRC-77 scrambler radio, which weighed thirty pounds with its battery. They shared the weight of memory. They took up what others could no longer bear. Often, they carried each other, the wounded or weak. They carried infections. They carried chess sets, basketballs, Vietnamese-English dictionaries, insignia of rank, Bronze Stars and Purple Hearts, plastic cards imprinted with the Code of Conduct. They carried diseases, among them malaria and dysentery. They carried lice and ringworm and leeches and paddy algae and various rots and molds. They carried the land itself—Vietnam, the place, the soil—a powdery orange-red dust that covered their boots and fatigues and faces. They carried the sky. The whole atmosphere, they carried it, the humidity, the monsoons, the stink of fungus and decay, all of it, they carried gravity.

They moved like mules. By daylight they took sniper fire, at night they were mortared, but it was not battle, it was just the endless march, village to village, without purpose, nothing won or lost. They marched for the sake of the march. They plodded along slowly, dumbly, leaning forward against the heat, unthinking, all blood and bone, simple grunts, soldiering with their legs, toiling up the hills and down into the paddies and across the rivers and up again and down, just humping, one step and then the next and then another, but no volition, no will, because it was automatic, it was anatomy, and the war was entirely a matter of posture and carriage, the hump was everything, a kind of inertia, a kind of emptiness, a dullness of desire and intellect and conscience and hope and human sensibility. Their principles were in their feet. Their calculations were biological. They had no sense of strategy or mission. They searched the villages without knowing what to look for, not caring, kicking over jars of rice, frisking children and old men, blowing tunnels, sometimes setting fires and sometimes not, then forming up and moving on to the next village, then other villages, where it would always be the same. They carried their own lives. The pressures were enormous. In the heat of early afternoon, they would remove their helmets and flak jackets walking bare, which was dangerous but which helped ease the strain. They would often discard things along the route of march. Purely for comfort, they would throw away rations, blow their Claymores and grenades, no matter, because by nightfall the resupply choppers would arrive with more of the same, then a day or two later still more, fresh watermelons and crates of ammunition and sunglasses and woolen sweaters—the resources were stunning—sparklers for the Fourth of July, colored eggs for Easter. It was the great American war chest—the fruits of science, the smokestacks, the canneries, the arsenal at Hartford, the Minnesota forests, the machine shops, the vast fields of corn and wheat— they carried like freight trains; they carried it on their backs and shoulders—and for all the ambiguities of Vietnam, all the mysteries and unknowns, there was at least the single abiding certainty that they would never be at a loss for things to carry.

After the chopper took Lavender away, Lieutenant Jimmy Cross led his men into the village of Than Khe. They burned everything. They shot chickens and dogs, they trashed the village well, they called in artillery and watched the wreckage, then they marched for several hours through the hot afternoon, and then at dusk, while Kiowa explained how Lavender died, Lieutenant Cross found himself trembling.

He tried not to cry. With his entrenching tool, which weighed five pounds, he began digging a hole in the earth.

He felt shame. He hated himself. He had loved Martha more than his men, and as a consequence Lavender was now dead, and this was something he would have to carry like a stone in his stomach for the rest of the war.

All he could do was dig. He used his entrenching tool like an ax, slashing, feeling both love and hate, and then later, when it was full dark, he sat at the bottom of his foxhole and wept. It went on for a long while. In part, he was grieving for Ted Lavender, but mostly it was for Martha, and for himself, because she was a junior at Mount Sebastian College in New Jersey, a poet and a virgin and uninvolved, and because he realized she did not love him and never would.

Like cement, Kiowa whispered in the dark. I swear to God—boom-down. Not a word.

I've heard this, said Norman Bowker.

A pisser, you know? Still zipping himself up. Zapped while zipping.

All right, fine. That's enough.

Yeah, but you had to see it, the guy just—

I *heard*, man. Cement. So why not shut the fuck *up*?

Kiowa shook his head sadly and glanced over at the hole where Lieutenant Jimmy Cross sat watching the night. The air was thick and wet. A warm, dense fog had settled over the paddies and there was the stillness that precedes rain.

After a time Kiowa sighed.

One thing for sure, he said. The Lieutenant's in some deep hurt. I mean that crying jag—the way he was carrying on—it wasn't fake or anything, it was real heavy-duty hurt. The man cares.

Sure, Norman Bowker said.

Say what you want, the man does care.

We all got problems.

Not Lavender.

No, I guess not, Bowker said. Do me a favor, though.

Shut up?

That's a smart Indian. Shut up.

Shrugging, Kiowa pulled off his boots. He wanted to say more, just to lighten up his sleep, but instead he opened his New Testament and arranged it beneath his head as a pillow. The fog made things seem hollow and unattached. He tried not to think about Ted Lavender, but then he was thinking how fast it was, no drama, down and dead, and how it was hard to feel anything except surprise. It seemed unchristian. He wished he could find some great sadness, or even anger, but the emotion wasn't there and he couldn't make it happen. Mostly he felt pleased to be alive. He liked the smell of the New Testament under his cheek, the leather and ink and paper and glue, whatever the chemicals were. He liked hearing the sounds of night. Even his fatigue, it felt fine, the stiff muscles and the prickly awareness of his own body, a floating feeling. He enjoyed not being dead. Lying there, Kiowa admired Lieutenant Jimmy Cross's capacity for grief. He wanted to share the man's pain, he wanted to care as Jimmy Cross cared. And yet when he closed his eyes, all he could think was Boom-down, and all he could feel was the pleasure of having his boots off and the fog curling in around him and the damp soil and the Bible smells and the plush comfort of night.

After a moment Norman Bowker sat up in the dark.

What the hell, he said. You want to talk, *talk*. Tell it to me.

Forget it.

No, man, go on. One thing I hate, it's a silent Indian.

For the most part they carried themselves with poise, a kind of dignity. Now and then, however, there were times of panic, when they squealed or wanted to squeal but couldn't, when they twitched and made moaning sounds and covered their heads and said Dear Jesus and flopped around on the earth and fired their weapons blindly and cringed and sobbed and begged for the noise to stop and went wild and made stupid promises to themselves and to God and to their mothers and fathers, hoping not to die. In different ways, it happened to all of them. Afterward, when the firing ended, they would blink and peek up. They would touch their bodies, feeling shame, then quickly hiding it. They would force themselves to stand. As if in slow motion, frame by frame, the world would take on the old logic—absolute silence, then the wind, then sunlight, then voices. It was the burden of being alive. Awkwardly, the men would reassemble themselves, first in private, then in groups, becoming soldiers again. They would repair the leaks in their eyes. They would check for casualties, call in dust-offs, light cigarettes, try to smile, clear their throats and spit and begin cleaning their weapons. After a time someone would shake his head and say, No lie, I almost shit my pants, and someone else would laugh, which meant it was bad, yes, but the guy had obviously not shit his pants, it wasn't that bad, and in any case nobody would ever do such a thing and then go ahead and talk about it. They would squint into the dense, oppressive sunlight. For a few moments, perhaps, they would fall silent, lighting a joint and tracking its passage from man to man, inhaling, holding in the humiliation. Scary stuff, one of them might say. But then someone else would grin or flick his eyebrows and say, Roger-dodger, almost cut me a new asshole, *almost*.

There were numerous such poses. Some carried themselves with a sort of wistful resignation, others with pride or stiff soldierly discipline or good humor or macho zeal. They were afraid of dying but they were even more afraid to show it.

They found jokes to tell.

They used a hard vocabulary to contain the terrible softness. *Greased,* they'd say. *Offed, lit up, zapped while zipping.* It wasn't cruelty, just stage presence. They were actors and the war came at them in 3-D. When someone died, it wasn't quite dying, because in a curious way it seemed scripted, and because they had their lines mostly memorized, irony mixed with tragedy, and because they called it by other names, as if to encyst and destroy the reality of death itself. They kicked corpses. They cut off thumbs. They talked grunt lingo. They told stories about Ted Lavender's supply of tranquilizers, how the poor guy didn't feel a thing, how incredibly tranquil he was.

There's a moral here, said Mitchell Sanders.

They were waiting for Lavender's chopper, smoking the dead man's dope.

The moral's pretty obvious, Sanders said, and winked. Stay away from drugs. No joke, they'll ruin your day every time.

Cute, said Henry Dobbins.

Mind-blower, get it? Talk about wiggy—nothing left, just blood and brains.

They made themselves laugh.

There it is, they'd say, over and over, as if the repetition itself were an act of poise, a balance between crazy and almost crazy, knowing without going. There it is, which meant be cool, let it ride, because oh yeah, man, you can't change what can't be changed, there it is, there it absolutely and positively and fucking well *is.*

They were tough.

They carried all the emotional baggage of men who might die. Grief, terror, love, longing—these were intangibles, but the intangibles had their own mass and specific gravity, they had tangible weight. They carried shameful memories. They carried the common secret of cowardice barely restrained, the instinct to run or freeze or hide, and in many respects this was the heaviest burden of all, for it could never be put down, it required perfect balance and perfect posture. They carried their reputations. They carried the soldier's greatest fear, which was the fear of blushing. Men killed, and died, because they were embarrassed not to. It was what had brought them to the war in the first place, nothing positive, no dreams of glory or honor, just to avoid the blush of dishonor. They died so as not to die of embarrassment. They crawled into tunnels and walked point and advanced under fire. Each morning, despite the unknowns, they made their legs move. They endured. They kept humping. They did not submit to the obvious alternative, which was simply to close the eyes and fall. So easy, really. Go limp and and tumble to the ground and let the muscles unwind and not speak and not budge until your buddies picked you up and lifted you into the chopper that would roar and dip its nose and carry you off to the world. A mere matter of falling, yet no one ever fell. It was not courage, exactly; the object was not valor. Rather, they were too frightened to be cowards.

By and large they carried these things inside, maintaining the masks of composure. They sneered at sick call. They spoke bitterly about guys who had found release by shooting off their own toes or fingers. Pussies, they'd say. Candyasses. It was fierce, mocking talk, with only a trace of envy or awe, but even so, the image played itself out behind their eyes.

They imagined the muzzle against flesh. They imagined the quick, sweet pain, then the evacuation to Japan, then a hospital with warm beds and cute geisha nurses.

They dreamed of freedom birds.

At night, on guard, staring into the dark, they were carried away by jumbo jets. They felt the rush of takeoff. *Gone!* they yelled. And then velocity, wings and engines, a smiling stewardess—but it was more than a plane, it was a real bird, a big sleek silver bird with feathers and talons and high screeching. They were flying. The weights fell off, there was nothing to bear. They laughed and held on tight, feeling the cold slap of wind and altitude, soaring, thinking *It's over, I'm gone!*—they were naked, they were light and free—it was all lightness, bright and fast and buoyant, light as light, a helium buzz in the brain, a giddy bubbling in the lungs as they were taken up over the clouds and the war, beyond duty, beyond gravity and mortification and global entanglements—*Sin loi!* they yelled, *I'm sorry, motherfuckers, but I'm out of it, I'm goofed, I'm on a space cruise, I'm gone!*—and it was a restful, disencumbered sensation, just riding the light waves, sailing that big silver freedom bird over the mountains and oceans, over America, over the farms and great sleeping cities and cemeteries and highways and the Golden Arches of McDonald's. It was flight, a kind of fleeing, a kind of falling, falling higher and higher, spinning off the edge of the earth and beyond the sun and through the vast, silent vacuum where there were no burdens and where everything weighed exactly nothing. *Gone!* they screamed, *I'm sorry but I'm gone!* And so at night, not quite dreaming, they gave themselves over to lightness, they were carried, they were purely borne.

On the morning after Ted Lavender died, First Lieutenant Jimmy Cross crouched at the bottom of his foxhole and burned Martha's letters. Then he burned the two photographs. There was a steady rain falling, which made it difficult, but he used heat tabs and Sterno to build a small fire, screening it with his body, holding the photographs over the tight blue flame with the tips of his fingers.

He realized it was only a gesture. Stupid, he thought. Sentimental, too, but mostly just stupid.

Lavender was dead. You couldn't burn the blame.

Besides, the letters were in his head. And even now, without photographs, Lieutenant Cross could see Martha playing volleyball in her white gym shorts and yellow T-shirt. He could see her moving in the rain.

When the fire died out, Lieutenant Cross pulled his poncho over his shoulders and ate breakfast from a can.

There was no great mystery, he decided.

In those burned letters Martha had never mentioned the war, except to say, Jimmy, take care of yourself. She wasn't involved. She signed the letters "Love," but it wasn't love, and all the fine lines and technicalities did not matter.

The morning came up wet and blurry. Everything seemed part of everything else, the fog and Martha and the deepening rain.

It was a war, after all.

Half smiling, Lieutenant Jimmy Cross took out his maps. He shook his head hard, as if to clear it, then bent forward and began planning the day's march. In ten minutes, or maybe twenty, he would rouse the men and they would pack up and head west, where the maps showed the country to be green and inviting. They would do what they had always done. The rain might add some weight, but otherwise it would be one more day layered upon all the other days.

He was realistic about it. There was that new hardness in his stomach.

No more fantasies, he told himself.

Henceforth, when he thought about Martha, it would be only to think that she belonged elsewhere. He would shut down the daydreams. This was not Mount Sebastian, it was another world, where there were no pretty poems or midterm exams, a place where men died because of carelessness and gross stupidity. Kiowa was right. Boom-down, and you were dead, never partly dead.

Briefly, in the rain, Lieutenant Cross saw Martha's gray eyes gazing back at him.

He understood.

It was very sad, he thought. The things men carried inside. The things men did or felt they had to do.

He almost nodded at her, but didn't.

Instead he went back to his maps. He was now determined to perform his duties firmly and without negligence. It wouldn't help Lavender, he knew that, but from this point on he would comport himself as a soldier. He would dispose of his good-luck pebble. Swallow it, maybe, or use Lee Strunk's slingshot, or just drop it along the trail. On the march he would impose strict field discipline. He would be careful to send out flank security, to prevent straggling or bunching up, to keep his troops moving at the proper pace and at the proper interval. He would insist on clean weapons. He would confiscate the remainder of Lavender's dope. Later in the day, perhaps, he would call the men together and speak to them plainly. He would accept the blame for what had happened to Ted Lavender. He would be a man about it. He would look them in the eyes, keeping his chin level, and he would issue the new SOPs in a calm, impersonal tone of voice, an officer's voice, leaving no room for argument or discussion. Commencing immediately, he'd tell them, they would no longer abandon equipment along the route of march. They would police up their acts. They would get their shit together, and keep it together, and maintain it neatly and in good working order.

He would not tolerate laxity. He would show strength, distancing himself.

Among the men there would be grumbling, of course, and maybe worse, because their days would seem longer and their loads heavier, but Lieutenant Cross reminded himself that his obligation was not to be loved but to lead. He would dispense with love; it was not now a factor. And if anyone quarreled or complained, he would simply tighten his lips and arrange his shoulders in the correct command posture. He might give a curt little nod. Or he might not. He might just shrug and say Carry on, then they would saddle up and form into a column and move out toward the villages west of Than Khe.

Study Questions

1. Discuss the concept of power in Huddle's "The Interrogation of the Prisoner Bung by Mister Hawkins and Sergeant Tree." Who seems to be in power? Who really is?

2. What kind of man is Mister Hawkins? Analyze his character and his response to his position as an interrogator.

3. Discuss the imagery in Baber's "The Ambush." What do the grasshoppers represent? What does the color white seem to symbolize?

4. Discuss the impact of revealing Thi Bong Dzu's age at the very end of Rottmann's story.

5. How does Susan's attitude change by the end of Grau's "Homecoming"? Why is she finally able to join the people inside?

6. Analyze the writing style in Heinemann's "The First Clean Fact." What are its characteristics and what is the tone or effect achieved by its intense, musical, colloquial language?

7. At the end of Wolff's "Wingfield," why does the narrator drink to the bats, crickets, locusts and cicadas? What is the significance of the snoring earth, nodding trees and dreaming narrator?

8. In O' Brien's "The Things They Carried," what is the significance of the statement "He [Cross] would dispense with love; it was not now a factor?"

9. What is the effect of O'Brien's cataloging all the things the soldiers carried?

10. Compare and contrast the way the soldier's experience is presented in "The Things They Carried" and "The First Clean Fact."

12. Compare and contrast the narrators (both of whom are now out of the war) in "The Ambush" and "Wingfield."

Drama

Drama is different from other forms of fiction in that it is written to be performed, not read. Rather than assimilating printed words, the audience is expected to hear the words and watch them being spoken; different senses are used than in the appreciation of poetry or short stories. Also, a greater immediacy is generated in drama because the audience must move along with the action, with little time to pause or mull over the events taking place. Drama rarely offers long descriptive passages, direct insight into the characters' thoughts, or analysis of their behavior unless it is specifically talked about by one of the characters. The characters in a play must speak, gesture, and behave in such a way as to hold the audience's attention, keep the plot moving and reveal the author's central concept or theme—all at the same time, all through dialogue.

One problem arises when a play is read rather than seen: no director has interpreted the piece (possibly in collaboration with its creator) so the reader's imagination must work overtime, designing a stage set, dressing the actors and directing their movements. In their heads, readers must visualize the characters; even if general descriptions are given in the script, each reader will imagine a slightly different shape of the nose or turn of the lips. The way the fatigues blouse over the boots, a laugh that dies into a snicker, a slouch with one leg flung over the arm of a flower print wing-backed chair—all can be subject to the whims and wishes of a reader's mind. The reader becomes director and audience simultaneously, perhaps imposing a bit of his or her own psyche and personality on the piece.

Of course some scripts never get into production so their interpretations remain in the minds of their readers. Others are written for television, others for the movies.

Vietnam War films made their most notable debut with the movie version of Robin Moore's *The Green Berets* (Warner Brothers, 1968), then swung around to less heroic, more introspective films such as *The Deer Hunter* (United Artists, 1978) directed by former Green Beret Michael Cimino, and *Apocalypse Now* (Zoetrope/United Artists 1979) Francis Ford Coppola's retelling of Joseph Conrad's *Heart of Darkness*. The mid 1980s show a renewed interest in Vietnam War movies; most successful to date is Oliver Stone's *Platoon* (Orion, 1987). Television has produced

97

several fine films, most based on actual experiences, such as *Friendly Fire* (ABC TV, Marble Arch Productions/Starger, 1979) which is C.D.B. Bryan's account of Peg and Gene Mullen's frustrating search for the truth about their son's death. *Unnatural Causes* (NBC TV, 1986) told the story of Maude De Victor's fight for Veteran's Administration recognition of Agent Orange-related health problems.

In general, however, plays about the Vietnam War have been less popular and successful than movie or television productions. Obviously the theatre is less capable of recreating a believable combat scenario, even if William Shakespeare set an early precedent for war plays in *Henry the Fifth*, when he managed to "cram Within this wooden O the very casques That did affright the air at Agincourt" (Prologue, 12-14). Instead of making grand demands on their audiences' imaginations, many modern playwrights focus their dramas either on the aftereffects of the war, as in Lanford Wilson's *The 5th of July* or on surreal representations of the war experience, as in David Rabe's trilogy containing *The Basic Training of Pavlo Hummel, Sticks and Bones* and *Streamers*.

These plays are probably the most complex and creative written so far, based on a few central concepts. First of all, each play presents a vision of an America that is permanently poisoned by the war. Second, the physically or psychologically wounded veteran is shown ironically as a painful, horrible embarrassment because he represents the ruin of America's myth of heroism and goodness. Furthermore, these plays offer an image of the American spirit as a thin veneer of euphemisms and patriotic rhetoric. Finally, the Vietnam War—its ambiguity, confusion, wreckage—is presented as a strong entity which exists beyond its land boundaries in Southeast Asia. Vietnam is a tension and a memory which pulses inside each American who fought in the war, waited to be sent to it, protested it, supported it, or watched it on television.

David Rabe
Streamers
1970

David Rabe was born in 1950 in Dubuque, Iowa. He served in the U.S. Army from 1965-1967, including a tour of duty in Vietnam. In 1970 Rabe won an Associated Press Award for a series of articles on drug rehabilitation; he has also won an Obie Award, Drama Desk Award, Drama Guild Award, Antoinette Perry Award and New York Drama Critics Circle Award. Among his works are "The Orphan;" In The Boom Boom Room; *and his Vietnam trilogy,* The Basic Training of Pavlo Hummel, Sticks and Bones, *and* Streamers.

Streamers *is set in a large cadre room of stateside army barracks. The soldiers who live there are completing their basic training, awaiting assignment. Vietnam looms before them, but their image of it is derived either from rhetoric they've heard about it or from a horrific projection of their imaginations. Carlyle is an angry draftee, Richie—a wealthy neurotic. Roger, street wise, and Billy, midwestern and patriotic, also comprise the central core of characters whose suppressed rage surfaces as their personalities clash and as their future is endangered by the war.*

Carlyle: Oh, man, I hate this goddamn army. I hate this bastard army. I mean, I just got outa basic—off leave—you know? Back on the block for two weeks—and now here. They don't pull any a that petty shit, now, do they—that goddamn petty basic training bullshit? They do and I'm gonna be bustin' some head—my hand is gonna be upside all kinds a heads, 'cause I ain't gonna be able to endure it, man, not that kinda crap—understand?
(And again, he is rushing at ROGER.)
Hey, hey, oh, c'mon, let's get my wheels and make it, man, do me the favor.

Roger: How'm I gonna? I got my obligations. (And CARLYLE spins away in anger.)

Carlyle: Jesus, baby, can't you remember the outside? How long it been since you been on leave? It is so sweet out there, nigger; you got it all forgot. I had such a sweet, sweet time. They doin' dances, baby, make you wanna cry. I hate this damn army. (The anger overwhelms him.)
All these mother-actin' jacks givin' you jive about what you gotta do and what you can't do. I had a bad scene in basic—up the hill and down the hill; it ain't somethin' I enjoyed even a little. So they do me wrong here, Jim, they gonna be sorry. Some-damn-body! And this whole Vietnam THING—I do not dig it. (He falls on his knees before ROGER. It is a gesture that begins as a joke, a mockery. And then a real fear pulses through him to nearly fill the pose he has taken.)
Lord, Lord, don't let 'em touch me. Christ, what will I do, they DO! Whoooooooooooooo! And they pullin' guys outa here, too, ain't they? Pullin' 'em like weeds, man; throwin' 'em into the fire. It's shit, man.

Roger: They got this ole sarge sleeps down the hall—just today they got him.

Carlyle: Which ole sarge?

Roger: He sleeps just down the hall. Little guy.

Carlyle: Wino, right?

Roger: Booze hound.

Carlyle: Yeh; I seen him. They got him, huh?

Roger: He's goin'; gotta be packin' his bags. And three other guys two days ago. And two guys last week.

Carlyle: (Leaping up from BILLY'S bed) Ohhh, them bastards. And everybody just takes it. It ain't our war, brother. I'm tellin' you. That's what gets me, nigger. It ain't our war nohow because it ain't our country, and that's what burns my ass—that and everybody just sittin' and takin' it. They gonna be bustin' balls, man—kickin' and stompin'. Everybody here maybe one week from shippin' out to get blown clean away and, man, whata they doin'? They doin' what they told. That what they doin'. Like you? Shit! You gonna straighten up your goddamn area! Well, that ain't for me; I'm gettin' hat, and makin' it out where it's sweet and the people's livin'. I can't cut this jive here, man. I'm tellin' you. I can't cut it.

(He has moved toward ROGER, and behind him now RICHIE enters, running, his hair wet, traces of shaving cream on his face. Toweling his hair, he falters, seeing CARLYLE. Then he crosses to his locker. CARLYLE grins at ROGER looks at RICHIE, steps toward him and gives a little bow.)
    My name is Carlyle; what is yours?

Richie: Richie.

*   *   *

Billy: How long you think we got?

Roger: What do you mean?
    (Roger is hanging up the mops; BILLY is now kneeling on ROGER's bunk.)

Billy: Till they pack us up, man, ship us out.

Roger: To the war, you mean? To Disneyland? Man, I dunno; that up to them IBM's. Them machines is figurin' that. Maybe tomorrow, maybe next week, maybe never.
(The war—the threat of it—is the one thing they share.)

Richie: I was reading they're planning to build it all up to more than five hundred thousand men over there. Americans. And they're going to keep it that way until they win.

Billy: Be a great place to come back from, man, you know? I keep thinkin' about that. To have gone there, to have been there, to have seen it and lived.

Roger: (Settling onto BILLY's bunk, he lights a cigarette.) Well, what we got right here is a fool, gonna probably be one a them five thousand, too. Do you know I cry at the goddamn anthem yet sometimes? The flag is flyin' at a ball game, the ole Roger gets all wet in the eye. After all the shit been done to his black ass. But I don't know what I think about this war. I do not know.

Billy: I'm tellin' you, Rog—I've been doin' a lot a readin' and I think it's right we go. I mean, it's just like when North Korea invaded South Korea or when Hitler invaded Poland and all those other countries. He just kept testin' everybody and when nobody said no to him, he got so committed he couldn't back out even if he wanted. And that's what this Ho Chi Minh is doin'. And all these other Communists. If we let 'em know somebody is gonna stand up against 'em, they'll back off, just like Hitler would have.

Roger: There is folks, you know, who are sayin' L.B.J. is the Hitler, and not ole Ho Chi Minh at all.

Richie: (Talking as if this is the best news he's heard in years) Well, I don't know anything at all about that, but I am certain I don't want to go—whatever is going on. I mean, those Vietcong don't just shoot you and blow you up, you know. My God, they've got these other awful things they do: putting elephant shit on these stakes in the ground and then you step on 'em and you got elephant shit in a wound in your foot. The infection is horrendous. And then there's these caves they hide in and when you go in after 'em, they've got these snakes that they've tied by their tails to the ceiling. So it's dark and the snake is furious from having been hung by its tail and you crawl right into them— your face. My God.

Billy: They do not.
(Billy knows he has been caught; they all know it.)

Richie: I read it, Billy. They do.

Billy: (Completely facetious, yet the fear is real) That's bullshit, Richie.

Roger: That's right, Richie. They maybe do that stuff with the elephant shit, but nobody's gonna tie a snake by its tail, let ole Billy walk into it.

Billy: That's disgusting, man.

Roger: Guess you better get ready for the Klondike, my man.

Billy That is probably the most disgusting thing I ever heard of. I DO NOT WANT TO GO! NOT TO NOWHERE WHERE THAT KINDA SHIT IS GOIN' ON! L.B.J. is Hitler; suddenly I see it all very clearly.

Roger: Billy got him a hatred for snakes.

Richie: I hate them, too. They're hideous.

Billy: (And now, as a kind of apology to RICHIE, BILLY continues his self-ridicule far into the extreme.) I mean, that is one of the most awful things I ever heard of any person doing. I mean, any person who would hang a snake by its tail in the dark of a cave in the hope that some other person might crawl into it and get bitten to death, that first person is somebody who oughta be shot. And I hope the five hundred thousand other guys that get sent over there kill 'em all—all them gooks— get 'em all driven back into Germany, where they belong. And in the meantime, I'll be holding the northern border against the snowmen.

Roger: (Rising from BILLY's bed) And in the meantime before that, we better be gettin' at the ole area here. Got to be strike troopers.

Billy: Right.

Lanford Wilson
The 5th of July
1978

In 1937 Lanford Wilson was born in Lebanon, Missouri. He began writing plays while still in school as San Diego State College and the University of Chicago. Among many others, his works include The Gingham Dog, Lemon Sky *and* The Hot 1 Baltimore *which won Critics, Obie and Outer Circle Awards. Wilson has also received Rockefeller, Guggenheim and Yale fellowships.*

Ken Talley, the central figure in The 5th of July, *has two artificial legs replacing those he lost in Vietnam. The drama is set at his house, a farm near Lebanon, Missouri, where Ken and his lover, Jed, are visited by Ken's sister June, niece Shirley, aunt Sally, and three friends, Gwen, John and Weston. As Ken and his friends remember the freedom and idealism they felt together in the early sixties, they must each come to terms with what they have separately become since then. The excerpted lines here follow a question posed by John and Gwen as to whether or not Ken is going to teach at their former high school.*

Ken: Oh, hardly, no. The profession has done very nicely without me for six years. I think it will survive a while longer.

Gwen: I thought that's what you were down here for. You were going back to your old high school.

Ken: I was never that interested in teaching.

Sally: Oh, you were so.

Gwen (overlapping Sally): You used to scream about it all the time.

John: Hell you weren't. That was your mission, I thought.

Ken: Well, once again, Super Fag's plans fail to materialize.

John: That guy said you were the best teacher Oakland ever had.

Ken: Would you get off my back? That's all I hear from Jed and Sally and June. I don't need it from you. Yes, I was quite happy leaving our cozy abode in Oakland each morning, and walking briskly into the Theodore Roosevelt High School. Very "Good Morning, Miss Dove," very "Goodbye, Mr. Chips," And—by prancing and dancing and sleight of hand, I actually managed to get their attention off sex for one hour a day. They became quite fascinated by trochees. But I'm afraid anymore my prancing would be quite embarrassing to them.

John: So you're afraid, so you'll get over it.

Ken: So everyone tells me.

June: Running like a rabbit would be closer—

Ken: Fear has nothing to do with it. As I slowly realized that no accredited English department was interested in my stunningly over-qualified application, except the notoriously parochial hometown...

June: Fine, that's where you belong.

Ken: ...I became aware that what everyone was trying to tell me was—that teaching impressionable teenagers in my present state, I could only expect to leave quite the wrong impression. You have no idea how much noise I make falling down.

John: Oh, bull. A big-deal War Hero. They'd love you.

Ken: I don't think so. And though it seems incredible to us, they don't even know where Vietnam is.

June: Why don't you just admit you're vain and terrified and face it instead of—

Ken: I have simply developed an overpowering distaste for chalk.

Study Questions

1. In Rabe's *Streamers,* what contradictions are apparent between Carlyle's words and his actions?

2. How would you characterize Billy's assessment of the war in Vietnam?

3. What is Billy's reaction to Richie's story about the tied snakes? Why does he react this way?

4. What can you determine about Ken's personality from this excerpt from Wilson's *The 5th of July?*

5. Discuss what this brief passage tells us about how the Vietnam War veteran was regarded after the war.

Poetry

Many people think the words 'poetry' and 'war' come close to being a contradiction of terms. To such people, 'poetry' conjures up images of delicately metered lines, describing in lilting rhymes and subtle metaphors the splendor of nature or the wonder of love. Other readers, those who may acknowledge that poetry need be neither rhymed nor beautiful, still resist the notion of war poetry because writing about war seems too political, and politics and art don't mix. Fortunately, such opinions prove little more than the naivete of the people who voiced them. There is a long, fine tradition of war poetry in the United States, and the poetry written about Vietnam continues that tradition with a new resonance.

Although we rarely use poetry to celebrate battles, as the early Greeks or the Medieval knights did, contemporary war poetry is alive, well, politically persuasive and artistically noteworthy. W.D. Ehrhart's simple words in "The Invasion of Grenada" have a strength far greater than the oratorical pomposity of a political rally. And John Balaban's subtle image of Vietnamese heritage in "For Miss Tin in Hue" is unquestionably rich.

In fact, poetry is well suited to commenting on the surrealistic nature of war, be it jungle combat or military life in a foreign environment. This is because the essence of poetry is vivid imagery and a compression of meaning. It would be difficult to put in one paragraph of prose the stories of an exploding mine, the desire to become a man, permanent sterility, the irony of war's attraction, and a bitter longing for death. Yet Basil T. Paquet's "Basket Case" does all this, wrenching the reader into an awareness of the startling set of associations between war, manhood, birth and death.

Poetry can often say more than prose, making words work overtime in double meanings and triple meanings. Using figurative language such as metaphors, similes and personification, poetry makes comparisons, forming sights, smells and textures for the reader to experience. In addition, the rhythms and tones of poetry reveal even more. For example, the narrator of Michael Casey's "Road Hazard" speaks to us in a casual, detached way that is deeply disturbing once his twisted sensibilities become apparent. And the precise sonnet form of Stephen Sossaman's

"A Viet Cong Sapper Dies" focuses attention on the final couplet whose hushed tone simmers with religious irony.

Certainly poets manipulate the denotation and connotation of words. When the veteran writes of the "heat" of Vietnam, he or she may be speaking of the searing temperatures or the intensity of combat. In its denotation, "night" is obviously the opposite of day, but the connotation varies. For many people, night means rest and security, but for the infantryman in the bush, nighttime meant an impenetrable darkness, Viet Cong sappers, hordes of mosquitoes, and a mandatory silence in which the snap of a twig would close the throat and set the heart pounding. Thus the vitality of this poetry comes from the efficiency with which the writers use their language. Choosing words carefully and assembling images which range from the rank odor of sweat-stained fatigues to the dazzling spectrum of jungle greens, poets can capture the sensory experiences of Vietnam and help their readers understand why those experiences were terrifying or confusing or exhilarating.

Some of the Vietnam War poetry written by Americans is too stripped down, too isolated in a single voice. And often the solitary voice seems to have as its only poetic resource the cataloging of firefight rubble and soldiers' cynical gestures. However, there are many poets who have transcended the obvious monsoon-across-the-paddies imagery, avoided repetitious graphic descriptions of death and have written forceful, meditative verse. Some of these poems are sad, angry, hopeful or mocking. Still others are elusive in tone, forcing the reader into an emotional response. Nearly all of the poems, however, depict war as a violation of social expectations and natural order. Hence war and poetry can mix, and the result demands that the reader explore the correspondence that poetry creates between the mind and the written image.

Denise Levertov
"What Were They Like?"
1966

Denise Levertov was born in Ilford, Essex, England, in 1923, and served as a nurse during World War II. After marrying American writer Mitchell Goodman, she came to the United States where she became a citizen in 1955. Along with writing, Levertov teaches English at Stanford University. Among others, her books include Overland to the Islands, With Eyes at the Back of Our Heads, Here and There, Jacob's Ladder, The Sorrow Dance, *and* Oblique Prayers.

What Were They Like?

1.) Did the people of Vietnam
    use lanterns of stone?
2.) Did they hold ceremonies
    to reverence the opening of buds?
3.) Were they inclined to quiet laughter?
4.) Did they use bone and ivory,
    jade and silver, for ornament?
5.) Had they an epic poem?
6.) Did they distinguish between speech and singing?

1.) Sir, their light hearts turned to stone.
    It is not remembered whether in gardens
    stone lanterns illumined pleasant ways.
2.) Perhaps they gathered once to delight in blossom,
    but after the children were killed
    there were no more buds.
3.) Sir, laughter is bitter to the burned mouth.
4.) A dream ago, perhaps. Ornament is for joy.
    All the bones were charred.
5.) It is not remembered. Remember,
    most were peasants; their life
    was in rice and bamboo.

When peaceful clouds were reflected in the paddies
and the water buffalo stepped surely along terraces,
maybe fathers told their sons old tales.
When bombs smashed those mirrors
there was time only to scream.
6.) There is an echo yet
of their speech which was like a song.
It was reported their singing resembled
the flight of moths in moonlight.
Who can say? It is silent now.

John Balaban
"For Miss Tin in Hue"—1971
"The Guard at the Binh Thuy Bridge"—1974

After finishing graduate school at Harvard University, John Balaban went to Vietnam as a conscientious objector with the International Voluntary Services. While there he served as a field representative for the Committee of Responsibility to Save War-Injured Children and as a teacher of linguistics at the University of Can Tho in the Mekong Delta. In 1971 Balaban returned to Vietnam to study and collect the oral folk poems of Vietnamese farmers. Balaban is the author of several books of poetry, including After Our War *and* Blue Mountain; *translation; and a recent novel,* Coming Down Again. *He teaches at Pennsylvania State University.*

For Miss Tin in Hue

The girl (captured; later, freed)
and I (cut by a centimeter of lead)
remember well the tea you steeped
for us in the garden, as music played
and the moon plied the harvest dusk.
You read the poem on a Chinese vase
that stood outside your father's room,
where he dozed in a mandarin dream
of King Gia Long's reposing at Ben Ngu.
We worry that you all are safe.
A house with pillars carved in poems
is floored with green rice fields;
and roofed by all the heavens of this world.

The Guard at the Binh Thuy Bridge

How still he stands as mists begin to move,
as morning, curling, billows creep across
his cooplike, concrete sentry perched mid-bridge
over mid-muddy river. Stares at bush-green banks
which bristle rifles, mortars, men—perhaps.
No convoys shake the timbers. No sound
but water slapping boatsides, banksides, pilings.
He's slung his carbine barrel down to keep
the boring dry, and two banana-clips instead of one
are taped to make, now, forty rounds instead
of twenty. Droplets bead from stock to sight;
they bulb, then strike his boot. He scrapes his heel,
and sees no boxbombs floating towards his bridge.
Anchored in red morning mist a narrow junk
rocks its weight. A woman kneels on deck
staring at lapping water. Wets her face.
Idly the thick Rach Binh Thuy slides by.
He aims. At her. Then drops his aim. Idly.

Jan Barry
"Floating Petals"—1972
"In the Footsteps of Genghis Khan"—1982
"A Nun in Ninh Hoa"—1983

Born in Ithaca, New York, in 1943, Jan Barry attended the SUNY College of Forestry at Syracuse University then served with the 18th Avn. Co., U.S. Army Support Group in Vietnam, 1962-1963. Appointed from the enlisted ranks to the Corps of Cadets at the U.S. Military Academy, he resigned from West Point in November, 1964, in order to write in disagreement with U.S. policy in Vietnam, and was honorably discharged from active duty in 1965. Barry was a co-founder and national president of the Vietnam Veterans Against the War. As a journalist and freelance writer he has contributed to several poetry anthologies and written numerous commentaries published in The Bergen Record, The New York

Times, The Washington Post, *and other newspapers and magazines. Barry is the editor of* Peace Is Our Profession, *a co-editor of* Winning Hearts and Minds: War Poems by Vietnam Veterans, *and the author of* War Baby *and* Veterans Day.

Floating Petals

See: here, the bougainvillea;
there, the cactus and palm—
    here: the lotus flower:
    there, the bomb-shattered bamboo

of viet-nam

severed flowers, sharded fronds:
    floating in shrapnel,
    sealed in napalm.

In the Footsteps of Genghis Khan

There, where a French legionnaire
once walked patrol
around the flightline perimeter of the airfield
at Nhatrang
ten years later I walked
an American foreign expeditionary forces
soldier on night guard duty
at Nhatrang
occupied even earlier
twenty years before
(a year more than my nineteen)
by the Japanese

Unhaunted by the ghosts, living and dead
among us
in the red-tile roofed French barracks
or listening in on the old Japanese telephone line
to Saigon
we went about our military duties
(setting up special forces headquarters)
where once a French foreign legion post had been)
oblivious of the irony

of Americans walking in the footsteps
of Genghis Khan

Unencumbered by history
our own or that of 13th-century Mongol armies
long since fled or buried
by the Vietnamese
in Nhatrang, in 1962, we just did our jobs
replacing kepi's with berets, "ah so" with "gawd!"

A Nun in Ninh Hoa

It was quite a sight for a boy from Tennessee:
a Buddhist nun dressed in fire
sitting proudly amid a solemn, silent crowd,
flames and a smoke plume her terrible costume.

Riding shotgun on a fuel truck convoy,
"just along for the ride,"
Jimmy Sharpe saw a sight this morning
beyond any experience he can describe.

She sat smiling as though mocking the flames.
Her hands, held together in prayer,
slowly parted. Suddenly, she drooped,
sat up, then wilted in the fire.

Safe back at the base, Jimmy's chatter
circled the nightmare he still could taste.
He grinned—shivered—then softly swore
"Jeesus! How'd we get in this crazy place?"

Michael Casey
"Road Hazard"—1972
"The POW and the Hoi Chanh Rallier"—1972

*Michael Casey served in Vietnam from 1969-1970 in the Americal
Division with the Military Police as a highway patrolman on Vietnamese
National Highway One. His short stories and poetry have appeared in
many publications including* The Little Magazine, The Nation, The

Bellingham Review, The Nantucket Review, *and* College English. *His first book, a collection of poems, is entitled* Obscenities.

Road Hazard

Eddie throws an old poncho
We found   on the ruins of LZ Gator
Over most of it
And then he grabs
The more solid looking leg
And drags it to the side of the road
I pick up the loose hand
A right hand
That is still warm
Because of the sun
And go to the side of the road
To tuck it
Under the right side
Of the poncho
With my being a Cong Giao
I think of making the sign
Of the cross but don't
Want to appear weak
To my public   the Nuoc Mau
Citizens standing around this scene
Holding their noses
We   Eddie and I
Go back to the jeep
Where Hieu was waiting all this time
With a handkerchief over his nose
I still am having
What poker face I have on
But Hieu still pats me on the shoulder
And says   okay   okay   no sweat no sweat
And I'm put out that
He doesn't do likewise to Eddie
Maybe I did appear the weakling

The Pow Cage and the
Hoi Chanh Rallier

The Chieu Hoi
Walks through the gate
With Dutch behind him
Dutch's M-sixteen on his hip
And at the door of the shack
Bagley gives a great big smile
And yells welcome
Throwing his arms out wide
Then Bagley goes and shakes
The kid's hand
And the Chieu Hoi
Gets the happiest look on his face
This kid has just seen Santa
Bagley portraying Santa here
The kid doesn't really understand Bagley
The kid doesn't understand English
But for us
Bagley keeps on with his act
    Now
    I'll tell ya what I'm gonna do
    Kid
    If ya play ya cards right
    Ya can be a Kit Carson scout
    And be a point man
    For the United States Grunts
    And
    While that might be fun
    I kindly fuckin doubt it
    But
    It's just another one
    Of the many bennies
    In today's action army
    Hey
    Kid
    This fuckin army's allll right

W.D. Ehrhart
"Hunting"—1972
"A Relative Thing"—1972
"Invasion of Grenada"—1984

Born in 1948, W.D. Ehrhart studied at Swarthmore College and the University of Illinois at Chicago Circle. He enlisted in the Marines in 1966 and was sent to Vietnam in 1967 where he served as Assistant Intelligence Chief with the 1st Bn., 1st Marines. After his service, Ehrhart became active in the Vietnam Veterans Against the War and was a co-editor of Demilitarized Zones *and a contributing editor to* Those Who Were There *and* Carrying The Darkness. *Besides teaching, Ehrhart has continued to write; his other works include* Vietnam-Perkasie, To Those Who Have Gone Home Tired, *and* Marking Time. *His prose and poetry have appeared in many periodicals such as* Tri-Quarterly, The Chronicle of Higher Education *and* The Virginia Quarterly Review. *He has received grants and awards from the Academy of American Poets, The Mary Roberts Rinehart Foundation and the Pennsylvania Council on the Arts.*

Hunting

Sighting down the long black barrel,
I wait till front and rear sights
form a perfect line on his body,
then slowly squeeze the trigger.

The thought occurs
that I have never hunted anything in my whole life
except other men.

But I have learned by now
where such thoughts lead,
and soon pass on
to chow, and sleep,
and how much longer till I change my socks.

A Relative Thing

We are the ones you sent to fight a war
you didn't know a thing about.

It didn't take us long to realize
the only land that we controlled
was covered by the bottoms of our boots.

When the newsmen said that naval ships
had shelled a VC staging point,
we saw a breastless woman
and her stillborn child.

We laughed at old men stumbling
in the dust in frenzied terror
to avoid our three-ton trucks.

We fought outnumbered in Hue City
while the ARVN soldiers looted bodies
in the safety of the rear.
The cookies from the wives of Local 104
did not soften our awareness.

We have seen the pacified supporters
of the Saigon government
sitting in their jampacked cardboard towns,
their wasted hands placed limply in their laps
their empty bellies waiting for the rice
some district chief has sold
for profit to the Victcong.

We have been Democracy on Zippo raids
burning houses to the ground,
driving eager amtracs through new-sown fields.

We are the ones who have to live
with the memory that we were the instruments
of your pigeon-breasted fantasies.
We are inextricable accomplices
in this travesty of dreams:
but we are not alone.

We are the ones you sent to fight a war
you did not know a thing about—
those of us that lived
have tried to tell you what went wrong.
Now you think you do not have to listen.

Just because we will not fit
into the uniforms of photographs

of you at twenty-one
does not mean you can disown us.

We are your sons, America,
and you cannot change that.
When you awake,
we will still be here.

The Invasion of Grenada

I didn't want a monument,
not even one as sober as that
vast black wall of broken lives.
I didn't want a postage stamp.
I didn't want a road beside the Delaware
River with a sign proclaiming:
"Vietnam Veterans Memorial Highway."

What I wanted was a simple recognition
of the limits of our power as a nation
to inflict our will on others.
What I wanted was an understanding
that the world is neither black-and-white
nor ours.

What I wanted
was an end to monuments.

Gustav Hasford
"Bedtime Story"—1972

Gustav Hasford was born in 1947 and served in the U.S. Marine Corps from 1966-1968. He was in Vietnam from 1967-1968 as a combat correspondent with Task Force X-Ray, 1st Marine Division. An early member of the Vietnam Veterans Against the War, Hasford is the author of The Short-Timers *(1979), a novel which is also the basis for Stanley Kubrick's 1987 film,* Full Metal Jacket. *Currently Hasford lives and writes in Perth, Western Australia.*

Bedtime Story

Sleep, America.
Silence is a warm bed.
Sleep your nightmares of small
    cries cut open now
    in the secret places of
Black Land, Bamboo City.

Sleep tight, America
    dogtags eating sweatgrimaced
    TV-people
Five O'clock news: My son the Meat.

Laughing scars, huh?
    Novocained fist.
Squeeze every window empty
    then hum.

Fear only the natural unreality
    and sleep on a pillow of blood
    and kiss nostalgia goodbye
Bayonet teddy bear and snore.
Bad dreams are something you ate.
    So sleep, you mother.

Basil T. Paquet
"Basket Case"—1972
"Christmas '67"—1972
"Easter '68"—1972

Basil T. Paquet, born in 1944, served as a medic in the U.S. Army, with service in Vietnam from 1967-1968 with the 24th Evac Hospital. A writer of short stories and poems, Paquet is co-founder of the 1st Casualty Press, and a contributor and co-editor of Winning Hearts and Minds: War Poems by Vietnam Veterans *and* Free Fire Zone: Short Stories by Vietnam Veterans.

Basket Case

I waited eighteen years to become a man.
My first woman was a whore off Tu Do street,
But I wish I never felt the first wild
Gliding lust, because the rage and thrust
Of a mine caught me hip high.
I felt the rip at the walls of my thighs,
A thousand metal scythes cut me open,
My little fish shot twenty yards
Into a swamp canal.
I fathered only this—the genderless bitterness
Of two stumps, and an unwanted pity
That births the faces of all
Who will see me till I die deliriously
From the spreading sepsis that was once my balls.

Christmas '67

Flares lit the night like a sky
Full of Bethlehem stars.
Dark wings against a darker sky
Laid down red ribbons and bars
Of bright crashing metal
To warn of the on-coming
Assault of men, the long battle
Filled with cries of "in-coming,"
That sent them crawling about
Into the pocked earth, waiting for the promise
Of thudding hosannas, like a gathering of devout
Moths, aching for the flames, but frozen by the hiss
And whistle of mortars and rockets sliding
Down their air pews in a choiring of dying.

Easter '68

I have seen the pascal men today.
Long past rising to a passion
they sucked their last sun
through blued lips,
buttressed their intestines in handfuls,
lifting their wounds to the sky
they fell silent as the sun,

as words not spoken,
broken Easters of flesh
girdled in fatigue strips,
red arching rainbows of dead men
rising like a promise
to give Jesus the big kiss
and sinking down—
only my breath on their lips,
only my words on their mouths.

Walter McDonald
"For Kelly, Missing in Action"—1973
"Hauling Over Wolf Creek Pass in Winter"—1984

Walter McDonald was born in 1934 in Lubbock, Texas. He was a pilot and instructor in the U.S. Air Force from 1957-1971, and served in Vietnam from 1969-1970. Currently McDonald is a professor of English at Texas Tech University and author of many works including Caliban in Blue, Burning the Fence, Anything, Anything, One Thing Leads to Another *and* Working Against Time. *His poems appear in* Tri-quarterly, Poet Lore, Quartet *and many other magazines and journals.*

For Kelly,
Missing in Action

When you disappeared
over the North
I pulled down Dubliners.

What strange counterparts,
you and the Cong.
You, who said no one would make
General
reading Joyce,
named your F-4 "The Dead,"
and dropped out of the sun
like some death angel
playing mumbledy peg
with bombs.

I never knew what launched
the search for Araby in you,
that wholly secular search
for thrills.

Hauling Over Wolf Creek Pass in Winter

If I make it over the pass
I park the rig, crawl back to the bunk
and try to sleep, the pigs swaying
like a steep grade, like the last curve
Johnson took too fast and burned.
But that was summer. His fire
spread to the next county.

It doesn't worry me.
I take the east climb no sweat
and the rest is a long coasting
down to the pens in Pagosa Springs.
It's the wolves I wait for.
We never see them any other way,
not in this business.
Sometimes five, six hauls before
propped on one arm, smoking,
I see them slink from the dark pines
toward the truck. They drive the pigs
crazy, squealing
as if a legion of demons had them.
Later, when I start up and go,
the pigs keep plunging,
trying to drive us over the cliff.

I let them squeal, their pig hearts
exploding like grenades.
The wolves are dark and silent.
Kneeling, I watch them split up
like sappers, some in the tree lines,
some gliding from shadow to shadow,
red eyes flashing in moonlight,
some farther off, guarding the flanks.
Each time, they know they have me.

I take my time, knowing I can crawl
over the seat, light up,
sip from the steaming thermos.
I crank the diesel,
release the air brakes
like a rocket launcher.
Wolves run in circles. I hit the lights.
Wolves plunge through deep snow
to the trees, the whole pack starving.
Revving up, the truck rolls down the highway
faster, the last flight out of Da Nang.
I shove into third gear, fourth,
the herd of pigs screaming, the load
lurching and banging on every turn,
almost delivered, almost airborne.

Stephen Sossaman
"Can Tho Family"—1975
"A Viet Cong Sapper Dies"—1980

Stephen Sossaman has received degrees from Columbia University and SUNY Stony Brook, and is a PhD candidate at New York University. In Vietnam, Sossaman served as an artillery Fire Direction Controller in the 9th Infantry Division, 1968, in the Mekong Delta. He is currently an assistant professor of English at Westfield State College and writes both poetry and fiction which are published in a variety of journals including Centennial Review *and* Cottonwood Review.

Can Tho Family

1.
Perplexed, a child
asks words from frowns:
a cough in a hushed temple.

2.
Two women light fires
and breathe slow smoke,
their trance a gift.

3.
In sleep Tran stares
through closed eyes:
full wombs, glowing.

4.
The moon swallows stars
and eats the night.

A Viet Cong Sapper Dies

Those Chu Lai priests who raised me as a boy,
Those earnest soldiers calling me a man,
All spoke of sacrifice as the great joy
And shamed my acquiescence in their plan.
Alone here, far from family, with no wife,
I crouch before my comrades' saving fire
And purchase others' deaths with this one life,
As with my bleeding palms I part the wire.
Compelled by love of others, quelling dread,
I fall upon the concertina wire,
And hang here hearing bullets at my head,
The screaming of an awesome, furied choir.
To those who led me softly to this wild,
Let linger this reproach: behold the child.

Bryan Alec Floyd
"Private Rex Jones, U.S.M.C."—1983
"Second Lieutenant Parvin Zelmer, U.S.M.C."—1983

Born in Oklahoma, Bryan Alec Floyd graduated from Seattle University in 1966. He served in the Marine Corps from 1966-1968, after which he taught high school and college English in Washington and Maryland. Floyd received an M.A. from Johns Hopkins University in 1974. He currently teaches at Suffolk County Community College on

Long Island. His works include The Long War Dead *and* Prayerfully Sinning.

Private Rex Jones, U.S.M.C.

Eighteen years old
and wild for war,
he volunteered.
After two weeks in Nam
he defined Eternity as a tour of duty:
thirteen months.
He was a born loser,
ghetto-born and raised,
a high school drop-out and finally a grunt,
but he defined *Forever*.
His definition was so utterly simple
even the Pentagon physicists
understood it.
When old Rex bought the farm
and was a hero,
he was buried in Arlington,
not far from the Kennedy brothers.
He joined half of his platoon there.
Several of us who came back
visited old Rex,
thinking we would say something.
None of us said a word.
Eighteen years old.

Second Lieutenant Parvin Zelmer, U.S.M.C.

The reason he died?
He and the platoon came upon
three Vietnamese children, ages three, five and eight,
who were playing with some tied-together pieces
of nice, shiny plastic that they had found in the grass.
The Lieutenant stood still
but ordered the rest of the platoon to fall back.
Then he asked the kids to put their toy,
a double booby trap, down gently,
but they did not understand

and pitched it to him,
and it bounced once and went boom,
gutting all four of them to shredded death.
A Congressman, upon hearing of the incident
from a news reporter,
asked the reporter one question:
"Was the booby-trap theirs or ours?"
And his question was the answer.

Michael O'Connor
"Night Dancing"—1984

Michael O'Connor served in Vietnam as a paratrooper with the 101st Airborne. Since then, his poetry has appeared in various journals including Cedar Rock, Pennsylvania Review, Voices International *and* Pig Iron Press. *O'Connor currently works as a regional manager for an auditing firm, teaches karate, and has competed on the kick-boxing circuit for a number of years.*

Night Dancing

1.
1963.
I was nine and riding in my father's '61 Impala,
all dark blue and big flat fins it cruised
sleek and silent up West Carson Street, a huge
metal hang glider cutting the night.
The radium dial on the dash board clock
spilled its sickly green glow over my father's lap,
his hands glowing and alien on the steering wheel.
It was then that I first noticed the house.
White, wooden, like a garden house it stood high above
West Carson Street gleaming like a white button on the
thread-bare suit of the W. W. Lawrence Paints Building.
The house seemed at once magical, almost sacred,
shining and white, a gleaming beacon high above Pittsburgh.
I asked my mom about it (no, THAT HOUSE, up there)
and she told me that the house *was* magical that
the rich and elite of the town held grand balls inside
very late at night, when no one else was awake,

and that the house was really much larger inside.
Every Sunday that summer we visited my Uncle Tom
in Castle Shannon. Coming home across the Fort Pitt Bridge
at night, I would crouch and scrunch myself into
a tight ball on the back-seat floor and lay my head
backwards on the seat, craning to look up through the back
window at the white house bright against summer night.
Colored lights from under the bridge reflected off the dark
Ohio River all shiny and strung so even like red and blue
glass bead necklaces, and I would close my eyes and dream
and the necklaces hung around the necks of long white women
with blonde hair and porcelain white gowns. I was older,
dressed in a proper suit and dancing on gleaming white
wood floors, and everyone loved me.

2.
1971.
This morning it is simply
the pattern my boots make standing on the floor
at the side of our small bed
that pleases me.
I roll over from the same dream of months,
see them, black leather shining dark,
Me Lei's delicate tatamis shy and small alongside
on the earthen floor of our hootch.
Me Lei is across the room at the hotplate.
In a thin, flowered robe she stands brewing the strong,
green tea whose name I never could pronounce.
Our hootch is less than two klicks off-base
yet today everything is quiet.
In my dream it always starts out like this.
Me Lei is brewing tea, I am just waking up
and there isn't a sound across the entire
101st Airmobile compound except a song I keep hearing
from an old movie. Stubby Kaye's voice drifts lazily
through the compound, our hootch:
"And the Devil will drag you under
by the sharp lapels of your checkered coat."
I go outside to see where the music is coming from
and the whistling starts. I know it is "Charlie" shelling
but there is no explosion, just the whistling getting louder
and louder and louder and I'm screaming incoming, incoming,
INCOMING! but it's too late and there is smoke and dirt

and wood hitting me in the face and I see Me Lei running
across the compound bleeding and screaming with no arms.
There is a small white hut across the compound gleaming
through the smoke and she is running toward the hut
and screaming at me, "Don't look at me, don't look at me."
A small girl follows her carrying Me lei's arms
in a bundle of rags. I am standing by the flag pole
dressed in a white tuxedo laughing.

This morning I look across the hootch at Me Lei,
her calligraphers ink hair cropped close below the nape
of her soft neck, shining warm, beckoning me back.

God, what I wouldn't give for a warm Pepsi and the sound
of Karen Carpenter's voice.

3.
We find out while on leave in Hue
that we are re-assigned from Pleiku
to Da Nang. "Charlie" is running hot there
and we are to support the 1st ARVN Division.
At night on patrol in Thang Binh
through the back swamps
the river water is as dark as the inside of your pocket.
The last three weeks have been spent in Huey Cobras
flying cover for "slicks."
Now, feet on the ground, trudging in single formation,
this earth feels wrong, a deep hole with no air.
When "Charlie" began shelling us
the world became dream-like and slow.
60mm shells lit up the sky in reds and blues,
all of the trees looked white against the flicker.
We lay in the mud, waiting crouched, anus clenched,
lost in a whirling dance
of night and flame
praying not to cry not to shit yourself,
not to ever get used to the waiting.
I remembered
my mom told me once that patience equaled growth
and that when I got older, if my patience had grown
with me I would be bigger inside because of it.
I still didn't know what in the hell that meant.
I just wanted to live to see twenty.

4.
1973.
Two years.
Two years and I still have the dreams.
Two years home, pretending I don't see
my mother's stares as she waits for me
to go over the edge again.
The pills don't work anymore and the doctors
never did.
I sit summer nights on the shore of the Ohio River,
my line baited for carp, symbol of nothing.
My body the burned out shell of a once white building.
The tugs go by, laugh their harsh laugh,
scatter colored necklaces like marbles.
I sit very still, eyes closed, listen to my dog tags
tick in the muggy breeze, watch my line not moving,
not moving. Another beer is what I need,
another beer another time another chance.
The line, not moving   not moving
and I am dancing alone on the Ohio's cement banks
laughing at the abandoned paint warehouse with its
stupid white house, laughing at my mother's stories,
at myself. At anyone who believes in anything good.
Reeling, I throw my rod into the black current,
set the hook down under my boot.
"How do you like it, lousy carp bastards!" I scream,
and laugh   and laugh   and laugh.

Bruce Weigl
"Song of Napalm"—1985

Bruce Weigl served in Vietnam from 1967-1968 with the 1st Air Cavalry. He taught creative writing at Old Dominion University, was an associate editor of Intervention *magazine, and currently teaches at Pennsylvania State University. His poetry collections include* Executioner, A Sackful of Old Quarrels, A Romance *and* The Monkey Wars. *Weigl is also editor of* The Imagination As Glory: The Poetry of James Dickey *and* The Giver of Morning: The Poetry of Dave Smith.

Song of Napalm
(for my wife)

After the storm, after the rain stopped pounding,
We stood in the doorway watching horses
Walk off lazily across the pasture's hill.
We stared through the black screen,
Our vision altered by the distance
So I thought I saw a mist
Kicked up around their hooves when they faded
Like cut-out horses
Away from us.
The grass was never more blue in that light, more
Scarlet; beyond the pasture
Trees scraped their voices into the wind, branches
Crisscrossed the sky like barbed wire
But you said they were only branches.

Okay. The storm stopped pounding.
I am trying to say this straight: for once
I was sane enough to pause and breathe
Outside my wild plans and after the hard rain
I turned my back on the old curses. I believed
They swung finally away from me...

But still the branches are wire
And thunder is the pounding mortar,
Still I close my eyes and see the girl
Running from her village, napalm
Stuck to her dress like jelly,
Her hands reaching for the no one
Who waits in waves of heat before her.

So I can keep on living,
So I can stay here beside you,
I try to imagine she runs down the road and wings
Beat inside her until she rises
Above the stinking jungle and her pain
Eases, and your pain, and mine.

But the lie swings back again.
The lie works only as long as it takes to speak
And the girl runs only as far
As the napalm allows

Until her burning tendons and crackling
Muscles draw her up

Into that final position
Burning bodies so perfectly assume. Nothing
Can change that; she is burned behind my eyes
And not your good love and not the rain-swept air
And not the jungle green
Pasture unfolding before us can deny it.

Wendy Wilder Larsen
"Chi Ai"—1986

Wendy Wilder Larsen was born in Boston in 1940, and she received a B.A. from Wheaton College and an M.A.T. from Harvard University. She lived in Saigon from 1970-1971 when her husband, a journalist, was sent there to cover the war. Larsen presently lives in New York City, and her poems have been published in Dark House, Hawaii Review, The Seattle Review, Tendril, 13th Moon, *and* Manhattan Poetry Review.

Chi Ai

Ai, the seamstress, was creepy.
She weighed as much as a mynah bird
and looked like one.
She could copy anything.
She stopped sewing
only to eat plain rice,
nothing on it.
She'd swish the last kernel
from her bowl
with cold brown tea.

My mother's words
floated up to me
like lyrics from some song.

    "Eat everything on your plate.
    Remember the starving children of China."

I was told this over bowls of oatmeal
brown sugar and heavy cream.
At the bottom of the dish,
Beatrix Potter's Peter Rabbit,
the prize for finishing.

Tran Thi Nga
"Photographs"—1986

Tran Thi Nga, born in China, 1927, attended Dong Khanh College, Hanoi and Swansea University in South Wales where she received a degree in Social Administration. In Saigon Nga was a social worker for the Ministry of Social Welfare, but fled to America when the city fell in 1975. In Vietnam and the U.S. Nga also worked for an American magazine; she now resides in Connecticut.

Photographs

We could bring only
what fit into one small bag.
They warned us not to take too much.
"They have things in the States,"
the Big Boss said.

For days I burnt documents on my terrace,
papers from when I worked for my government
papers from when I worked for the Americans.
I couldn't think
except to destroy whatever would bring trouble.

I burnt photographs
of the whole family at Tet,
year after year
all of us together
my father's nine birds.

I stared at the black-and-white pictures:
me—tiny, smiling
a pigtail on both sides
holding my eldest brother's hand,

me—the angel in the school play
a tiara on my head
me in China at the bottom of Sea Mountain
my children standing beside me.

As the pile of ashes floated away
I felt I was burning my life.

Study Questions

1. Compare the images of Vietnam in Levertov's "What Were They Like?"
   and Balaban's "For Miss Tin in Hue."

2. Discuss what Barry's "In the Footsteps of Genghis Khan" is saying
   about Vietnam's history and the men who have fought there.

3. Analyze the character of the speaker in Casey's "Road Hazard."

4. Discuss the tone of Ehrhart's "A Relative Thing" and the effect
   achieved by the repetition of "We are..." throughout the poem.

5. Explicate the disjointed images in Hasford's "Bedtime Story." To
   whom is the anger in this poem directed?

6. Analyze the interaction of the war, sex, birth and death images in
   Paquet's "Basket Case."

7. What subtle things does McDonald's "Hauling Over Wolf Creek Pass
   in Winter" say about the war in Vietnam?

8. Sossaman wrote "A Viet Cong Sapper Dies" in the form of a sonnet.
   Is the choice of this form ironic, or does it enhance the poem's
   meaning in some way?

9. Compare the two portraits, "Private Rex Jones" and "Second
   Lieutenant Parvin Zelmer" by Floyd.

10. The speakers of Weigl's "Song of Napalm" and O'Connor's "Night
    Dancing" both have a changed view of their life in America since
    their time in Vietnam. How do their attitudes or tones differ?

11. When Nga says in "Photographs," "I felt I was burning my life,"
    what does she mean? Won't she always have her memories?

13. For any of these poems, discuss how structure—line length, rhyme
    or no rhyme, stanza breaks, etc.—contributes to meaning.

14. In these poems, what references are made to wars or conflicts other than Vietnam?

15. Analyze how the language used in these poems helps express the poets' central themes.

Brief Time Line—
American Involvement in Vietnam

1950 (Jan) Ho Chi Minh declares that the Democratic Republic of Vietnam is the only legal government.

1950 The United States begins to subsidize the French presence in Vietnam. President Truman sends a 35-man military aid group.

1954 The U.S. supplies 80% of French war expenditures in Vietnam, but will not commit troops.

1954 (May) The Viet Minh, under command of General Vo Nguyen Giap, defeat the French army at Dien Bien Phu.

1954 (Jun) Colonel Edward G. Lansdale arrives in Saigon as head of U.S. military mission and then as CIA chief of station for domestic affairs.

1954 (Jul) Geneva Conference splits Vietnam along the 17th parallel into Communist North and non-communist South.

1955 Ngo Dinh Diem, backed by U.S., repudiates the Geneva Accords and organizes the Republic of Vietnam as an independent nation, with himself as president. The U.S. arms seven divisions of South Vietnamese with American weapons. (Jul) Ho Chi Minh accepts Soviet aid.

1957 (May) Diem visits the U.S. President Eisenhower confirms support for Diem's regime.

1960 (Dec) Hanoi leaders form the National Liberation Front (NLF) for South Vietnam, which Saigon dubs the "Vietcong," meaning Communist Vietnamese.

1961 U.S. build-up in South Vietnam begins. President Kennedy commits 16,000 advisers over the next two years to help defend South Vietnam.

1962 MACV (Military Assistance Command, Vietnam) is established.

1963 (Nov) Diem is assassinated by military junta. The U.S. recognizes the government of General Duong Van Minh. John F. Kennedy is assassinated. By the end of December 15,000 American military advisers are in South Vietnam.

1964 (Jan) General Nguyen Kahn seizes power from Minh. The U.S. recognizes the government of General Kahn. In July, South Vietnam begins covert maritime operations in the North.

1964 (Aug) Gulf of Tonkin incident. President Johnson orders the bombing of North Vietnam.

1965 (Mar) U.S. combat troops land at Da Nang. President Johnson increases the bombing of North Vietnam.

1965 (Jun) Air Vice Marshal Nguyen Cao Ky and Nguyen Van Thieu seize control of the Saigon government by military coup. Ky is appointed Chief of the executive committee.

1965 (Oct) American forces defeat North Vietnamese in the Ia Drang valley, the first large scale conventional confrontation of the war.

1966 U.S. troop strength in Vietnam exceeds 200,000. Buddhists demonstrate in Hue and Da Nang, protesting the war.

1967 (Jul) Vietcong attack the U.S. airbase in Da Nang.

1967 (Sep) General Thieu elected president of South Vietnam. U.S. troop strength exceeds 500,000.

1968 (Jan) Battle of Khe Sanh begins. The Tet offensive. The NLF attack major cities and towns in South Vietnam.

1968 (Mar) The My Lai massacre. President Johnson announces he will not run for re-election, and calls for peace talks with North Vietnam.

1968 (Nov) Johnson halts the bombing of North Vietnam.

1969 Peace talks begin in Paris, expanded to include the Vietcong and the Thieu government.

1969 (Sep) Ho Chi Minh dies.

1969 (Oct) Massive anti-war demonstrations in U.S. (Nov) Nixon announces Vietnamization plan; troop strength reduced by 60,000.

1970 (Apr) President Nixon announces the invasion of Cambodia by U.S. and South Vietnamese troops. Kent State and Jackson State killings.

1971 (Dec) U.S. troop strength below 160,000.

1972 Le Duc Tho and Henry Kissinger negotiate secretly. (Mar) Renewed bombing of Hanoi announced by Nixon, halted in Oct.

1973 (Jan) A peace agreement is signed in Paris. (Feb) First U.S. POW in North Vietnam is released. (Mar) The last U.S. troops leave Vietnam.

1975 (Apr) South Vietnam surrenders to North Vietnam. Saigon is renamed Ho Chi Minh City.

1982 (Nov) Dedication of the Vietnam Veterans Memorial in Washington, D.C.

Statistics

* The Vietnam War was the longest in United States' history.
* Approximately 2.7 million Americans served in this war.
* Approximately 58,000 Americans died or remain missing.
* Approximately 300,000 Americans were wounded.
* Approximately 600,000 Vietnamese soldiers died.
* Approximately 587,000 civilians died.
* Over one million Vietnamese fled their country.
* Nearly a half million Vietnamese immigrated to the U.S. after the fall of Saigon.
* The United States dropped approximately 7,600,000 tons of bombs on North Vietnam.
* 5.2 million acres of Vietnamese countryside were defoliated.
* The rough estimate of U.S. military expenditures between 1965 and 1973 for the war in Vietnam is over $120,000,000,000.

Glossary

AK-47:	NVA/VC assault rifle
amtrac:	an amphibious tractor, equipped with a machine gun
AO:	Area of Operations
APC:	Armored Personnel Carrier
arty:	artillery
ARVN:	Army of the Republic of Vietnam
bird:	helicopter
body count:	number of casualties inflicted in a firefight
boonierat:	infantryman
bouncing betty:	ground mine that explodes about waist high
C-4:	plastic explosive
CA:	Combat Assault
CAR-15:	carbine rifle
Charlie:	the Viet Cong
cherry:	new recruit
Chieu Hoi:	Vietnamese for Open Arms; program to encourage Communist desertions
Chinook:	CH-47 cargo helicopter
chopper:	helicopter
claymore:	anti-personnel mine used for defense and ambush
CO:	Commanding Officer
Cobra:	AG-1H assault helicopter
commo wire:	communications wire
Cong Giao:	Vietnamese for Catholic
CP:	Command Post
c-rats:	combat rations in cans
crispy critters:	reference to burn victims, usually the result of napalm
DEROS:	Date of Estimated Return from Overseas
dink:	(gook, slope) derogatory expression referring to the Vietnamese
dust-off:	medical evacuation by helicopter
firebase:	artillery firing position, secured by infantry

FNG:	Fucking New Guy
FO:	Forward Observer
frag:	(fragged, fragging) using a fragmentation hand grenade to kill or wound a person, usually referring to killing a superior officer or lifer
free fire zone:	area in which everyone is considered an enemy
freedom bird:	return flight to the United States
greased:	(wasted, zapped, blown away) killed or died
grunt:	infantryman
heat tabs:	inflammable tablets used for cooking c-rations
Hoi Chanh:	Communist deserter
hootch:	any dwelling, whether a home, bunker, or office
Huey:	UH-1 helicopter
hump:	hard work or heavy walking with a pack
in-coming:	receiving fire
in-country:	being in Vietnam
junk:	flat bottomed boat of Chinese design
KIA:	Killed in Action
Kit Carsen Scout:	enemy soldier who has changed sides, now working as an infantry scout
klick:	(click) a kilometer
LAW:	Light Anti-tank Weapon
laager:	defensive encampment
legs:	infantrymen
LRRP:	Long Range Reconnaissance Patrol
L-T:	Lieutenant
LZ:	Landing Zone
M-16:	automatic/semi-automatic assault rifle
M-60:	light machine gun
M-79:	single shot 40mm grenade launcher
Medevac:	medical evacuation by helicopter
mermite:	large insulated container
MIA:	Missing in Action
NVA:	North Vietnamese Army
Nam:	Vietnam
napalm:	jellied petroleum substance used

in flame throwers and bombs

O club:	officers' club
OP:	Observation Post
perimeter:	fortified boundary protecting a position
point:	first man in line on patrol
pop smoke:	mark a location by releasing a smoke grenade
Psy Ops:	Psychological Operations
pungi pit:	pit in which sharpened stakes tipped with manure or poison project upward
R & R:	Rest and Relaxation
Recon:	Reconnaissance unit
red ball:	enemy high speed road or trail
REMF:	Rear Echelon Mother Fucker
RPG:	Rocket Propelled Grenade
RTO:	Radio-Telephone Operator
rucksack:	standard issue infantry backpack
sapper:	NVA or VC soldier who infiltrates an allied base
short-timer:	person with a short time left to serve in Vietnam
slack:	second man in line on patrol
slick:	Huey helicopter
Snoopy:	forward air control; plane directing air strikes
SOP:	Standard Operating Procedure
stand down:	return to rear base for hot food, recreation and a brief rest
starlight scope:	device for night vision
Tet:	Vietnamese Lunar New Year; special reference to NVA/VC offensive during that holiday in 1968
thumper:	M-79 grenade launcher
TOC:	Tactical Operations Center
tracer:	rifle round which could be seen and traced
VC:	Viet Cong
WIA:	Wounded in Action
willy peter:	white phosphorous artillery round
World:	the United States or anywhere other than Vietnam
XO:	Executive Officer

zippo raids: burning of Vietnamese hootches while
                              on mission

Brief Bibliography

(This is by no means a complete bibliography; it is merely a list of suggested further readings. There are many fine novels, stories, plays and poems about the Vietnam War other than those included here.)

Novels

Baber, Asa. *The Land of a Million Elephants*. New York: Morrow, 1970.
Balaban, John. *Coming Down Again*. New York: Harcourt, Brace, Jovanovich, 1985.
Bunting, Josiah. *The Lionheads*. New York: Braziller, 1972.
Butler, Robert Olen. *The Alleys of Eden*. New York: Horizon Press, 1981.
———. *Sun Dogs*. New York: Horizon Press, 1982.
———. *On Distant Ground*. New York: Ballantine, 1985.
Del Vecchio, John. *The 13th Valley*. New York: Bantam, 1982.
Durden, Charles. *No Bugles, No Drums*. New York: Viking Press, 1976.
Eastlake, William. *The Bamboo Bed*. New York: Simon and Schuster, 1969.
Fuller, Jack. *Fragments*. New York: Morrow, 1984.
Greene, Graham. *The Quiet American*. New York: Viking Press, 1956.
Grey, Anthony. *Saigon*. Boston: Little Brown, 1982.
Halberstam, David. *One Very Hot Day*. Boston: Houghton Mifflin, 1967.
Hasford, Gustav. *The Short Timers*. New York: Harper & Row, 1979.
Heinemann, Larry. *Close Quarters*. New York: Farrar, Straus and Giroux, 1977.
———. *Paco's Story*. New York: Farrar, Straus & Giroux, 1986.
Hunter, R. Lanny, and Victor L. Hunter. *Living Dogs and Dead Lions*. New York: Viking, 1986.
Kalb, Bernard, and Marvin Kalb. *The Last Ambassador*. Boston: Little Brown, 1981.
Kolpacoff, Victor. *The Prisoners of Quai Dong*. New York: New American Library, 1967.
Lederer, William J., and Eugene Burdick. *The Ugly American*. New York: Norton, 1958.
Mailer, Norman. *Why Are We in Vietnam?* New York: Putnam, 1967.
Mason, Bobbie Ann. *In Country*. New York: Harper & Row, 1985.
Merkin, Robert. *Zombie Jamboree*. New York: Morrow, 1986.
Miller, Kenn. *Tiger the Lurp Dog*. Boston: Little, Brown, 1983.
Moore, Robin. *The Green Berets*. New York: Crown, 1965.
O'Brien, Tim. *Going After Cacciato*. New York: Delacorte Press/Seymour Lawrence, 1978.
Pelfrey, William. *The Big V*. New York: Liveright, 1972.
Pratt, John Clark. *The Laotian Fragments*. New York: Viking, 1974.
Proffitt, Nicholas. *Gardens of Stone*. New York: Carroll & Graf, 1983.
———. *Embassy House*. New York: Bantam, 1986.

Riggan, Bob. *Free Fire Zone*. New York, Norton, 1984.

Roth, Robert. *Sand in the Wind*. Boston: Little, Brown, 1973.

Rottman, Larry. *American Eagle: The Story of a Navajo Vietnam Veteran*. Madrid, New Mexico: Packrat Press, 1977.

Rubin, Jonathan. *The Barking Deer*. New York: Braziller, 1974.

Scott, Leonard. *Charlie Mike*. New York: Ballantine, 1985.

Sloan, James Park. *War Games*. Boston: Houghton Mifflin, 1971.

Stone, Robert. *Dog Soldiers*. Boston: Houghton Mifflin, 1974.

Tate, Donald. *Bravo Burning*. New York: Charles Scribner's Sons, 1986.

Webb, James H. *Fields of Fire*. Englewood Cliffs, New Jersey: Prentice-Hall, 1978.

———— *A Sense of Honor*. Englewood Cliffs, New Jersey: Prentice-Hall, 1981.

Wilson, William. *The LBJ Brigade*. Los Angeles: Apocalypse, 1966.

Winn, David. *Gangland*. New York: Knopf, 1982.

Wright, Stephen. *Meditations In Green*. New York: Charles Scribner's Sons, 1983.

Short Stories

Baber, Asa. *Tranquility Base and Other Stories*. Canton, New York: Fiction International, 1979.

Karlin, Wayne, Basil T. Paquet, and Larry Rottmann, eds. *Free Fire Zone: Stories by Vietnam War Veterans*. New York: McGraw-Hill, 1973.

Klinkowitz, Jerome and John Somer, eds. *Writing Under Fire: Stories of the Vietnam War*. New York: Dell, 1978.

Kumin, Maxin. *Why Can't We Live Together Like Civilized Beings?* New York: Viking, 1982.

Mayer, Tom. *The Weary Falcon*. Boston: Houghton Mifflin, 1971.

Drama

DiFusco, John. *Tracers*. New York: Hill & Wang, 1980.

Garson, Barbara. *Macbird*. Berkeley, California: Grassy Knoll Press, 1966.

King, Bruce. *Dustoff: A Play in Three Acts*. Sante Fe, New Mexico: Institute of American Indian Arts Press, 1982.

Kopit, Arthur. *Indians*. New York: Hill & Wang, 1969.

McNally, Terrence. *Botticelli*. In his *Apple Pie: Three One Act Plays*. New York: Dramatists Play Service, 1968.

Rabe, David. *The Basic Training of Pavlo Hummel*. New York: Samuel French, 1969.

———— *The Orphan*. New York: Samuel French, 1975.

———— *Sticks and Bones*. New York: Samuel French, 1972.

———— *Streamers*. New York: Knopf, 1973.

Terry, Megan. *Viet Rock*. New York: Simon and Schuster, 1967.

Wilson, Lanford. *The 5th of July*. New York: Dramatists Play Service, 1978.

Poetry

Balaban, John. *After Our War*. Pittsburgh: University of Pittsburgh Press, 1974.

———— *Vietnam Poems*. Oxford: Carcanet Press, 1970.

———, ed. and trans. *Ca Dao Vietnam: A Bilingual Anthology of Vietnamese Folk Poetry*. Greensboro, North Carolina: Unicorn Press, 1983.

Barry, Jan, and William Daniel Ehrhart, eds. *Demilitarized Zones: Veterans After Vietnam*. Perkasie, Pennsylvania: East River Anthology, 1976.

———, ed. *Peace is Our Profession: Poems and Passages of War Protest*. Montclair, New Jersey: East River Anthology, 1981.

Casey, Michael. *Obscenities*. New Haven: Yale University Press, 1972.

Ehrhart, William Daniel. *To Those Who Have Gone Home Tired*. New York: Thunder's Mouth, 1984.

——— *The Outer Banks and Other Poems*. East Hampton, Massachusetts: Adastra Press, 1984.

———, ed. *Carrying The Darkness*. New York: Avon, 1985.

Floyd, Bryan Alec. *The Long War Dead: An Epiphany, 1st Platoon, U.S.M.C.* New York: Avon, 1976.

Larson, Wendy and Tran Thi Nga. *Shallow Graves*. New York: Random House, 1986.

Mason, Steve. *Johnny's Song*. New York: Bantam, 1985.

McDonald, Walter. *Caliban in Blue and Other Poems*. Lubbock: Texas Tech Press, 1976.

Rottmann, Larry, Jan Barry, and Basil T. Paquet, eds. *Winning Hearts and Minds: War Poems by Vietnam Veterans*. New York: 1st Casualty Press-McGraw Hill, 1972.

Weigl, Bruce. *A Romance*. Pittsburgh: University of Pittsburgh Press, 1979.

Index

149